Edexcel 9-1 GCSE Business

TARGET 9-6

Revision Handbook for Top Grades

Ian Marcousé

 **A-Z** Business Training Ltd

Contents

Section 2: Key Theme 2 Concepts - Getting to Level 9

Section 3: Exam skills for top grades

Dynamic nature of business

What? (Grade 5 basics)

An old business saying is that 'if you're not going forwards you're going backwards'. This is because of constant change in technology, consumer taste and product line-ups. As a result of this dynamism, companies need always to be thinking about their next new product idea — and how to adapt their existing products to meet the changes in what people want.

Why? (Grade 6)

The two key factors at the heart of market dynamism are changes in technology and changes in what customers think they want. In the clothing business, fashion is an obvious driving force; and what is 'in fashion' must inevitably be out of fashion in the relatively near future. But in many other businesses fashion is also important. Carpet sales may be weak because the trend is for polished wooden floors; and sales of BBQs slump in a year with no World Cup and little sunshine.

How? (Grade 7)

The degree of dynamism in a market should ideally be measured. Chocolate sales in the UK have been around £3,000 million a year for a decade; new brands come and go; campaigners for better health come and won't go; but chocolate remains an amazingly stable, undynamic market in the UK. By comparison, the market for bicycles has been a sensation. Sales of bikes for adults have nearly doubled in the past ten years, with dramatic increases in the number of £1,000 bikes sold (and a probable wave of electric bikes to come). So chocolate is relatively undynamic; the market for cycling is very dynamic.

So? (Grade 8)

In dynamic markets companies must invest a lot in R&D and in market research. They must realise that product life cycles may be short. The annual launch of a new iPhone is testimony to Apple's investment of $billions each year on R&D. In less dynamic markets such as chocolate, relatively more money is spent advertising existing brands, such as Galaxy or Maltesers.

Grade 9

Companies such as Apple make huge efforts to hire young, dynamic people to match the dynamism of their technology-based marketplace. Fashion businesses do the same. So Human Resource departments may be especially important in fast-moving industries, to hire and hold the best young staff.

> **Do** think hard about the business story written by the examiner. Is this industry *really* dynamic? Or may it be relatively sleepy?

> **Don't** simplify technology into just I.T. Robots and drones are every bit as important as the internet. See the James Dyson product range to see the importance of technology.

> **Exam tip**: changes in consumer taste are important, but nothing 'disrupts' a market as dramatically as technology change.

Dynamic change: 5-step logic chain (necessary to get to the top response level)

Chain 1. A change in technology makes rival products look obsolete quite quickly (1) forcing those rivals to respond (2) … but if they haven't kept up with their own R&D spending they may be too far behind to catch up (3) … leaving them to cut costs to try to survive (4) … which may only make their problems worse, for example if they cut advertising and branding support (5)

Chain 2. Markets can be dynamic without technological change such as fashion clothing. (1) Here, designers come up with new ideas constantly, and keep finding willing customers (2) … who, at other times, would complain at the waste in resources resulting from this change (3) … but the planet somehow seems less important (4) when there are new clothes to be bought. (5)

Answering exams

There are several direct questions that an examiner can ask about dynamic market change. In addition the topic can be used to analyse many business situations and answer many high-mark questions

Here are three questions in which the dynamic nature of business can be a significant part of the answer. The first two are invented. The third is based on Edexcel's specimen papers.

Q1. Explain one disadvantage to a business if one of its products becomes obsolete. (3 marks)

Q2. XY Bakery plc is considering whether or not to increase substantially its spending on Research & Development. Justify whether or not it should increase its spending. (9 marks)

Q7e) Evaluate whether Sainsbury's is likely to benefit from its takeover of Home Retail Group. You should use the information provided as well as your knowledge of business. (12 marks)

On the right are strong answers to these three questions. They show the importance of understanding the dynamic nature of business – and also show how material from Theme 2 Building a Business can be used to develop answers to Theme 1 questions. Research & Development is a topic that builds on technology and is therefore very relevant to high-grade answers.

For more about exam technique see Section 3.

Grade 9 Answers (questions on left)

Q1. *Once a product is obsolete, it's too late to revive it. So the disadvantage is that its sales will be sliding towards the break-even output level. Once they slip below, the product will be a constant drain on profits – so it should be withdrawn.*

Q2. *Research and Development is essential – even for a bakery – when dynamic change is occurring in consumer eating habits. Recent years have seen a switch to flatbreads, as people prefer 'wraps' to sandwiches. Careful work would have been needed to find the right recipe for wraps to be used direct from the fridge, or defrosted from the freezer. R&D would also be involved in finding a recipe economical enough to help achieve high gross profit margins.*

In a business such as breadmaking there may be years when nothing much seems to be changing. There's still an argument, though, for active R&D that keeps looking at new ways to provide for the consumer – because being first to spot a new business opportunity is often the way to achieve huge success.

7e) *One reason for Sainsbury's move was its belief that Argos (part of the Home Retail Group) was significantly more advanced than Sainsbury's in its approach to online selling and delivery. In effect Sainsbury's wanted to buy up the work Argos had done on its online technology. Given the hugely tough competition Sainsbury's faced against giant Tesco and specialist online grocer Ocado, it was understandable that they wanted to buy themselves an edge.*

Despite this benefit, Sainsbury may be underestimating the other problems that can arise when a takeover takes place, such as disagreements between senior managers. The technology benefit may be outweighed by other managerial problems.

Overall, if Sainsbury's saw technology as a weakness, it is surely clever to tackle it by this takeover.

Risk and Reward

What? (Grade 5 basics)

Risk is the possibility that things will go wrong. It can be quantified, as in: 'there's only a 30% chance of success' and therefore a 70% chance of failure. Poor outcomes can lead to financial losses, lack of security or even the outright failure of a business.

Reward comes from the benefits of success. This might be in the form of profit - or from personal independence for the entrepreneur whose success provides control over his/her life.

Do think about the risks involved for that specific entrepreneur: has a family? Wealthy enough to take a loss?

Why? (Grade 6)

Entrepreneurs make decisions by weighing up risks compared with rewards. It might be worth taking a big risk if there's a possibility of a huge reward. In 2016 Skyscanner – a £100 start-up by 3 Scottish university students in 2001 – was bought for £1,400 million. So the reason why risk-reward matters is because it's a fundamental part of businesspeople's decision-making.

How? (Grade 7)

To judge risk against reward, you first need a numerical estimate of the level of risk. In the UK fewer than 1 in 5 new products becomes a success, so the risk of failure is 4 out of 5 (80%). But in a market such as healthy snacks, the reward for success can be sales of £20 million a year (Nakd cereal bars). So reward can be weighed against risk.

Don't be too inclined to avoid risk; business decisions are about the future, so every decision carries risk. Risk is not a bad thing; it's a fact of business life.

So? (Grade 8)

In the exam, never treat risk as a problem. In business risk is a factor to set against reward to make a judgement about whether or not to go ahead. All decisions are about the future, which introduces an element of risk. But as long as the rewards are good enough, risks are worth taking.

Grade 9

Risk has an ethical element as well. Me risking my money is my problem. But me risking other people's money may be their problem. An under-financed start-up may collapse at the cost of blameless customers and suppliers. They probably didn't realised the risks they were being encouraged to take. Good entrepreneurs take risk upon themselves; 'cowboys' impose risk on others.

Exam tip: it's easy to focus too much on risk (the downside). Balance your argument by writing clearly about reward as well.

Risk & Reward: 5-step logic chain (necessary to get to the top response level)

Chain 1. Both risk and reward can be measured or estimated (1) ... so they can be balanced against each other (2) ... which allows those with lots of capital to take big risks as long as the rewards are even bigger (3) . Businesspeople with less capital may accept that this risk is not for them (4) ... because they can't afford the losses involved if the idea fails (5)

Chain 2. Risk is caused by ignorance of customer wants. Nokia bet on buttons but the market wanted Apple's touchscreen. (1) ... To measure risk (and reward) market research is needed (2). This may lead to better decisions, which reduces risk (3) ... and may boost the levels of rewards available (4) which helps the business finance better long-term developments (5)

Answering exams

Edexcel produces sample exam papers to help teachers. In these there are only two 1-mark questions about risk. But in Edexcel's marking guidance there are far more references to risk. So risk is a concept that can be used to answer many different questions.

Here are three questions in which risk can be a significant part of the answer:

Q1d) Explain one disadvantage to a sole trader of having unlimited liability. (3 marks)

Q7d) Sally is considering whether or not to buy a franchise to start up on her own. Justify whether or not Sally should buy a franchise. (9 marks)

Q7e) Evaluate whether Sainsbury's is likely to benefit from its takeover of Home Retail Group. You should use the information provided as well as your knowledge of business. (12 marks)

So although a glance at the Sample Paper suggests there are only 2 marks relating to risk, in fact risk can be a significant part of answers to 26 marks' worth of questions. That makes risk (and reward) among the most important topics to revise.

On the right are strong answers to these three questions. They focus on how risk/reward can be used in the answers – so they are models for using risk/reward rather than models for how to score 9 or 12 marks.

For more on exam technique see Section 3.

Grade 9 Answers (questions on left)

1d) *Even for an apparently super-safe business, risks may arise from competition or from a poor economic climate. With unlimited liability the owner is responsible for all financial losses and debts, placing their personal/family finances at huge risk.*

7d) *Franchising works best when there's a powerful brand, marketed heavily and with clear operational benefits, such as McDonalds supplying the milkshake machines plus instructions. That's not the case here, with Sally offering a Personal Trainer service, which is about personal skill and stamina plus likeability/charisma.*

The risk for Sally is that she pays an upfront fee and signs an agreement taking 5% of her revenue without getting much in return. With a franchise, businesses don't usually go under, but they can merely 'exist', with too little profit for the franchisee. Sally would be taking on the risks, while the franchise owner enjoys the rewards.

7e) *Every takeover contains huge risks. The first is simple: caveat emptor - let the buyer beware. Buying a second hand car has the risk that the seller knows more about the car than you do; so it is with companies. Even if everything is great, the process of takeover has its own risks: especially that it may be hard to pull the two workforces together. Research shows this to be a bigger problem than managements expect. On the other hand the rewards may be so great that the risks are worth taking, as in the case of Whitbread buying Costa Coffee (50 stores then; 4,000 now). It's hard to see Sainsbury's buying Home Retail Group (Argos) in the same light. Yes, it may be helpful to tap in to the Argos online ordering and pick-up service, but perhaps Sainsbury's needs to get Online right all by itself.*

Are the potential rewards for Sainsbury's worth the risks? Not quite. Sainsbury's would've been better off focusing on a better Sainsbury's.

Adding Value

What? (Grade 5 basics)

Adding value means stretching the gap between the selling price and the cost of the materials used to make the item. The raw cocoa, sugar, milk and packaging materials in a small Cadbury's Dairy Milk cost 8p; the bar's selling price is 65p. So Cadbury has added 65p – 8p = 57p of value.

That 57p is not profit. Added value has to pay for labour, advertising and distribution costs before gross profit is calculated. Then head office fixed costs must be taken away to get to net profit.

Do think about how service businesses add value, such as the McD *Happy Meal* (that pathetic toy!) soon to reach its 40th birthday.

Why? (Grade 6)

If a business can add little or no value, it cannot last for long. It's easy to sell a lot of hamburgers if you use big beef patties made of £2 of top quality meat – and sell them for £2.50. But how will you pay the rent and the electricity bill? Adding value is the foundation of a business that will last.

How? (Grade 7)

Some businesses add value through their skills and innovativeness (think Jaguar Land Rover, JCB and James Dyson), perhaps based on great design and engineering. Others find cunning ways to achieve the same goal, by adding air to make products look bigger than they are (crisps, Aero and cosmetic jars with hollow bottoms), or dressing up an ordinary pair of jeans with a *Kardashian* logo. Brand names can add value as surely as good design.

Don't confuse added value with (gross) profit. Examiners will be impressed by any student who knows that added value is a stepping stone to profit, not the real thing.

So? (Grade 8)

In the exam, explain how different pathways can achieve the same outcome – higher value added can be achieved by high quality design or by little more than deception. It's up to the customer to decide whether a £1,000 price tag is money well spent, or a 'rip-off'. In the long term a business that does things brilliantly is likely to stay successful; adding value in a deceptive way may come unstuck.

Grade 9

When reading the business story on the exam paper, it's always useful to think about how the business adds value – and whether there is enough for long-term success. 'Jenny opens a hairdressing salon. There are four others nearby.' Your job is to ask whether Jenny has thought about how she will add value? And then whether there is a different approach she could take to help her charge a higher price for her service (one near me offers free dog-sitting!).

Exam tip: it's good to be sceptical of brands, e.g. the iPhone. Yes it's great, but £800+ of great? Is Apple's ability to add value making it greedy?

Adding value: 5-step logic chain (getting to the top response level)

Chain 1. A business needing to boost profit could start by building its added value (1) ... by cutting out parts of the service that customers place little value on (2) ... such as a fresh fish counter at a supermarket (3) ... and by cutting input costs (4) ... by working harder to eliminate waste (5).

Chain 2. For a jewellery business adding value is the key business idea (1) ... i.e. creating something of great value based on design, skill and high quality manufacture (2). Hiring better designers will be important in the long term (3) ... as they'll be able to create beautiful jewellery without having to use the most expensive materials (4)... therefore stretching the gap between price and materials cost (5)

Answering exam questions

Edexcel produces sample exam papers to help teachers. In these there is only one 3-mark question about adding value. But there are several other, longer questions in which adding value would add value to a student's answer. Here are three of them:

Q2d) Explain one method a business could use to add value to its product. (3 marks)

Q3e) Discuss what a small business owner should consider when deciding upon the location for their business. (6 marks)

Q6d) Neil and Sue are considering two options to reduce the amount they need to sell to break even.

Option 1: Increasing average prices by 10%.

Option 2: Reducing the cost of ingredients by using a cheaper supplier.

Justify which one of these two options Neil and Sue should choose. (9 marks)

So although a glance at the Specimen Paper suggests there are only 3 marks relating to adding value, in fact the topic can be a significant part of answers to many other questions.

On the right are strong answers to these three questions. They focus on how added value can be used in the answers – so they are models for using added value rather than models for how to score 9 or 12 marks

For more on exam technique see Section 3.

Grade 9 Answers (Qs. on the left)

2d) *It could use branding. By building a brand (using advertising and perhaps celebrity endorsement) customers might pick this product without looking for others to compare. This allows price increases that boost the value added.*

3e). *Especially for service businesses, location decisions must balance revenue against costs. Low-rent locations in a backstreet keep costs down but may make it very difficult to generate revenue. Convenience adds value, and locations in busy places (outside a busy station, perhaps) not only add to customer numbers but also allow prices to be increased. A dry cleaner at a station may charge 20% more than one in a backstreet, with commuters happy to pay up. The price increase can cover the higher rent, leaving extra customer numbers to boost profit.*

6d) *Neil and Sue should only consider a 10% price rise if they have found a way to add more value to their café products or service. Otherwise they might see a substantial fall in sales. There's no point in cutting the break-even point if sales fall below the new, lower, level. Possibly if they can eliminate customer queueing they could add value sufficiently to justify the price rise.*

With a cut in the cost of ingredients the only risk is that value may be deducted from the product if customers feel the effect of the cost-cutting. The impact of cheapening the product may be to make the café just like all the rest, which may mean losing loyal customers and – again – demand slipping below the new, lower, break-even point.

From the text it seems that Neil & Sue would hate to cut corners with the product or service; their satisfaction may be as important to them as their profit, making a price rise preferable to cost-cutting.

Entrepreneurship

What? (Grade 5 basics)

Entrepreneurship is the set of skills and attitudes that enable some people to put into practice ideas that others only dream about. The role of the entrepreneur includes taking risks, making business decisions and organising resources such as finance and staffing.

Why? (Grade 6)

Entrepreneurs set themselves apart by an optimistic outlook that makes them focus more on opportunities than threats. They usually find risk-taking exciting rather than scary. Perhaps it comes in part from curiosity, as in 'I wonder whether …?' Poet T.S. Eliot once said: 'Only those who will risk going too far can possibly find out how far it's possible to go.' So why do they do it? Because they love a challenge and are attracted to risk.

How? (Grade 7)

Some entrepreneurs stumble on the thing that makes them rich, such as Mark Zuckerberg at Facebook. Others look at a growing market and figure out how to find their own, successful place within it. Six years after ASOS began, Mahmud Kamani and Carol Kane founded Boohoo.com, another UK online fashion site. By its 10th birthday Boohoo was making £30 million profit per year. Some start up with pennies in the bank; others have wealthy families behind them. There are as many possibilities as there are start-ups.

So? (Grade 8)

When judging a start-up story featured in an exam, look not only at whether it went well but also at the circumstances of the entrepreneur. There is something especially impressive about those who started up with little or no money. Some will have risked their life savings (impressive) and some go further and risk the family house and stability (reckless!).

Grade 9

Grade 9 students see how concepts link together, such as entrepreneurship and risk/reward plus the links between section 1.1 Entrepreneurship and section 1.2 Spotting a Business Opportunity. This skill makes it much easier to construct a well-developed answer to the bigger, 12-mark evaluate questions. And these are the questions that swing the grades.

> **Do** think about the financial circumstances of the entrepreneur. Rich enough to cope with a loss? Or risking everything?

> **Don't** be too hard on an entrepreneur who's struggling at the start. There are so many balls to juggle with that it's understandable if some drop to the floor.

> **Exam tip:** keep a strong focus on the circumstances of the start-up, such as the actions of competitors and whether the business is really meeting customer wants.

Entrepreneurship: 5-step logic chain (to get to the top response level)

Chain 1. Most entrepreneurs seek to run a profitable business (1) … based on meeting customer needs (2). As every market is competitive, this needs a clever idea or a clever way to implement a standard idea (3). It is easy to think entrepreneurship is all about clever ideas and risk-taking (4), but it's also about organising resources to meet or beat customer needs and expectations (5).

Chain 2. A good entrepreneur takes an innovative idea (1) … that's focused on customer needs (2) … then raises the cash (3) to turn the idea into a great customer experience (4) … that keeps people coming back and encourages others to come and try (5).

Answering exams

Edexcel produces sample exam papers to help teachers. In these there are several questions about entrepreneurs. There are also broader questions in which a paragraph on enterprise would be very useful. Here are two questions set by the exam board:

Q2e) Explain **one** reason why an entrepreneur would produce a business plan. (3 marks)

Q7e) Evaluate whether Sally's business idea is likely to be a success. You should use the information provided as well as your knowledge of business. (12 marks)

On the right are strong answers to these two questions. They focus on how entrepreneurship can be used in the answers – and Q7e) can be regarded as a high-mark answer to a 12 mark question.

For more on exam technique see Section 3.

Grade 9 Answers (Qs. on the left)

2e) *A business plan is vital for an entrepreneur who needs to raise external capital, either from potential shareholders or in the form of a bank loan. The plan sets out expected short-term cash flows and forecast medium-term profit – both needed to help persuade financiers to invest.*

7e) Sally has started a business in the safest way possible: going from a fitness instructor to a fitness business means Sally is an expert in the field, knows what customers want and probably has clients to 'poach' from her former employer. No wonder she thinks she can charge higher prices per hour than her two rivals (Figure 6).

Is it likely to succeed? Apart from her start-up advantage, Sally has a strong business understanding of the need to differentiate herself from existing rivals and the right idea about matching a social media strategy to a young target audience. Every new business faces a high level of risk, but this seems to have a far better chance than most.

However, there are weaknesses. Sally is dithering about whether to buy a fitness franchise. This could only be necessary if she has no prospect of bringing existing clients with her. Furthermore she 'is currently well paid', so it will be hard for the venture to be worthwhile financially.

Sally should only go ahead if she's sure she can bring some clients with her – in which case there should be no need to buy a franchise.

Further Exam tip. All of Theme 1 is based on Investigating Small Business. Edexcel describes this as 'exploring core concepts through the lens of an entrepreneur setting up a business'. So the short business cases used in the exam will often be based on start-up (and therefore entrepreneurship).

Help prepare yourself for this by taking some interest in the start-up process, from Dragon's Den on BBC TV to re-reading the many stories your teachers will have used in class. Also, a useful (and free) online resource is www.startups.co.uk which has a super section on 'How They Started'.

Customer needs

What? (Grade 5 basics)

Customer needs include the right product of the right quality at an affordable price. Customers also need a wide range of choice (to suit their needs) and are willing to pay for convenience.

Why? (Grade 6)

It is important to identify and understand customer needs in order to generate sales and to help the business survive in a competitive world. If a business fails to understand the needs of its customers it is leaving itself exposed to attack from current or new competitors. If you're offering white sliced while your customers want organic wholemeal, you're in trouble.

How? (Grade 7)

To identify your customers it's hard to beat online registration. In a few moments you can find out your customers' age, address and gender. To understand them is harder, but can be done through qualitative market research. Many large companies run monthly surveys to measure any shifts in customer attitudes. This might show that customers no longer need to find low-fat foods, because their focus has shifted to low-carb.

So? (Grade 8)

It isn't easy to turn a business idea into big profits. To achieve success, nothing is more important than understanding your customers – and then focusing the business on meeting their needs. So it's important to monitor social media to keep listening to what's being thought and said about you.

Grade 9

At the highest level, unpick whether the issue is really customer *needs*. Isn't it really customer *wants*? In countries like Britain many people spend much of their income on wants rather than needs. I may tell myself 'I need a Snickers' but really I mean 'I want a Snickers'. Companies can be quite cunning at persuading us to buy more of what we don't need. So whereas companies might talk about their ability to meet customer needs, they often mean wants.

> **Do** consider that different people may have different needs – which may make it sensible to segment the market and offer different products

> **Don't** forget that customer needs are changing constantly, forcing companies to adapt existing products or launch new ones.

> **Exam tip:** customer needs are affected by their psychology, so qualitative research tends to be especially important.

Customer needs: 5-step logic chain (necessary to get to the top response level)

Chain 1. Customer needs can change with different fashions and trends (1) ... so businesses need to know what's happening on the street (2) ... then be bold about changing in line with trends (3) before new or existing rivals get there first (4) The more fashion-focused the market sector the more important this is. (5)

Chain 2. Companies sometimes hide behind the term customer needs, when they really mean 'wants' (1) ... In other words persuading customers to think they 'need' a new phone or a box of Lindor when they really just *want* one. (2) This means manipulating customers rather than serving them (3) ... possibly into buying things that are bad/fattening for them (4) which may be good business but is definitely questionable ethically. (5)

Market research - Purpose

What? (Grade 5 basics)

There are four main reasons why businesses spend their money and time on market research: to identify and understand customer needs; to identify gaps in the market; to provide the information needed to take business decisions and therefore reduce the risks involved.

Why? (Grade 6)

A shop owner running a bakery may deal with customers daily and know their likes and dislikes. A boss running a bigger, nation-wide business cannot meet all the customers, so market research is a way to keep in touch. The boss can read regular reports on customer comments, praise and complaints. And when big decisions have to be made, market research provides the information to help do the right thing.

How? (Grade 7)

Methods of carrying out market research can be grouped into primary and secondary. They are explained in the following chapter.

So? (Grade 8)

In business, you should never think in isolation. If company A is thinking about launching a new product or switching to e-commerce/online sales only, company B is probably thinking the same way. Market research is needed to give company A the edge: to help make a slightly better decision. The Sony PS4 wasn't that much better than the Xbox One – yet it's outsold XBox 2:1 globally.

Grade 9

The purpose of market research is to make better marketing decisions and therefore reduce the risk of failure. But fewer than 1 in 5 new products succeeds in the UK. Two years' after launch, 4 out of 5 have disappeared. Many will have used market research to help reduce the level of risk, but nothing can reduce that risk level to zero. Intelligent businesspeople use market research as an aid to decision-making, acting boldly where necessary, e.g. scrapping a new product before launch because the research findings are good – but not good enough.

> **Do** ask whether the business decision is important enough to justify spending £000s on market research. It's not always.

> **Don't** forget to match the purpose of the research to the method, e.g. if the purpose is background information, secondary research may be ideal.

> **Exam tip**: show the examiner you understand that small businesses often know their customers so well that there's no need to spend money on market research.

Market research purpose: 5-step logic chain (getting to the top response level)

Chain 1. If a company's sales are slipping it needs to find out why (1) ... so businesses need to find out what customers are thinking and where they're going (2) ... and the sooner the business can find out the quicker it can react (3) ... ideally before its competitors (4) When the business is clear on the purpose of the research it can think about the type of research needed, i.e. the research method. (5)

Chain 2. Market research is expensive and therefore needs to have a clear purpose (1) ... such as identifying whether a big enough gap exists in the market to enable a new product to be launched successfully. (2) This means finding out what consumers *really* want from this type of product (3) ... and where competitors are failing to provide what customers need or want. (4) If market research can unpick this information and helps launch a new product success, it'll be worth every penny. (5)

Market research: methods and use of data

What? (Grade 5 basics)

Market research methods can be grouped into two categories: primary and secondary. Primary research is carried out first-hand, asking selected people their views on topics a company wants answered directly, e.g. would you buy our new Orange Maltesers? Secondary research is second-hand, such as finding out from government statistics that the number of 15-19-year-olds in the UK is forecast to rise by 450,000 between 2020 and 2025. The data collected by research can be quantitative (statistical) or qualitative (psychological).

> **Do** consider whether the business needs psychological insights or numbers, e.g. to make a sales forecast.

Why? (Grade 6)

The different types of research do different jobs. If Ford decided to launch an electric-powered bike, it would need to find out general (secondary) information about the market for bikes e.g. what's the market size? What's the market growth? Then it might decide to discover more about the psychology of owning and choosing a bike; therefore it would use primary research in a qualitative way, perhaps using focus groups of 6 – 8 bike owners. Later on it might conduct a primary survey to get quantitative data to help forecast the likely level of sales for an electric bike (in Japan more than 500,000 'e-bikes' are sold each year, at over £500 each).

> **Don't** over-estimate the value of market research. Apple used no market research before launching its hugely successful iPad or iPhone. It believed it understood its customers well enough to know what they wanted.

How? (Grade 7)

Secondary research is done at your desk, probably starting with Google. Primary research must be done specifically, probably using an independent research company. Quantitative surveys can easily cost £10,000 and even small-scale qualitative research can cost £5,000+. A further issue here is how long? Primary research can take several weeks from start to final results – and some businesses worry about delays – especially when they're about to launch a new product.

So? (Grade 8)

Big decisions can make or lose a lot of money, so the choice of market research method is important. Some big businesses use research for every element of every decision. That's expensive and time-consuming, but can help prevent business disasters such as Samsung's launch of its Note 7 (the exploding one) or Cadbury's £4 million launch of 'Puddles' in 2015 – that's OK, no-one else remembers it. For Puddles, Cadbury used qualitative research that pointed towards young people as the target market. They weren't. Choosing the right method is vital.

> **Exam tip**: be firm in your conclusions about any data presented by the examiner. Too many students dither; top students are decisive – and give clear, firm reasoning for their decision.

Grade 9

Market research has to be reliable. That can only be achieved if the sample of people questioned is unbiased, i.e. truly represents people within the target market. For quantitative research there's another requirement – that the sample size should be big enough to give reliable data (perhaps 500-1,000 people). With reliability can come accuracy. And that enables marketing managers to draw clear conclusions – such as that the planned new product has a strong chance of succeeding. In the case of Cadbury and Puddles, that didn't happen.

Market research methods: 5-step logic chain (necessary for top response level)

Chain 1. For a new business start-up it's best to start with secondary research (1) … as lots is free and is available at public libraries and by Googling. (2) Having gained a broad understanding of the market an entrepreneur can focus on a specific market segment (3) … perhaps using primary research in the form of a qualitative focus group (4) … then use the insights gained to draw up a questionnaire to be used for quantitative research, then a sales forecast (5)

Chain 2. A famous business phrase is 'paralysis by analysis' (1) … which can happen when a business gathers so much market research information that managers struggle to reach a conclusion (2). This may lead to decisions being postponed because arrows pointing in one direction seem countered by others pointing elsewhere. (3) Market research should help in making decisions, not bog them down (4) … but this will only happen if the managers have clear objectives and the ability to be decisive. (5)

Answering exams

Edexcel produces sample exam papers to help teachers. In these there is only one 2-mark question about market research. But every exam contains a 9-mark question asking you to make a choice between 2 business options. Almost always, market research will form part of a good answer. See Q6d) below:

2 (a) Which two of the following are examples of primary market research?

Select two answers: (2)

A Internet research

B Market reports

C Customer survey

D Government statistics

E Focus group

Q6d) Neil and Sue are considering two options to reduce the amount they need to sell to break even.

Option 1: Increasing average prices by 10%

Option 2: Reducing the cost of ingredients by using a cheaper supplier

Justify which one of these two options Neil and Sue should choose. (9 marks)

On the right are strong answers to these two questions. The answer to Q6d shows how to use market research effectively.

For more on exam technique see Section 3.

Grade 9 Answers (questions on left)

2a) Correct answers: C and E

The other 3 are examples of secondary research sources

6d) A 10% price increase is a serious possibility. Neil and Sue's bakery and café 'has a lot of passing trade' and their traditional baking methods and high-quality ingredients are likely to give them a high degree of product (service) differentiation. Furthermore the text makes no mention of competition. With a revamp of the technology to reduce the queueing time, it's very possible that Meringue will end up with the same number of customers, but at 10% more revenue per sale.

By contrast, 'using a cheaper supplier' may put the whole business at risk. OK, it's conceivable that they've found someone to supply the same high-quality ingredients at a lower price, but surely it's more likely that the lower prices are due to lower standards. Customers used to quality can be unforgiving if standards slip.

If Neil and Sue are in doubt about what to do, the obvious solution is quantitative market research among existing customers. At the moment that will be easy to do: interview people as they queue. It seems overwhelmingly likely that Meringue regulars will opt for higher prices than a risk of slipping standards.

In the above answer, a 5-step logic chain is actually achieved in the first paragraph. Of course, the rest of the question has to be answered to achieve full marks.

Market Segmentation

What? (Grade 5 basics)

Segmentation means identifying the different customer groups within your market. A market can be segmented by age (young to old), by income (rich to poor), by lifestyle (trendy to traditional), by demographics (including gender and skin colour) or by location/geography (town to country or north to south).

Why? (Grade 6)

When a brand new product is launched, it may be designed to appeal to as many people as possible. But it probably can't be perfect for everyone. So, in the UK market for smartphones, there are phones designed for older customers (bigger buttons, fewer functions and simpler to operate). Segmentation can help expand the market size – some older people wouldn't bother with an ordinary smartphone but are happy to buy a simpler model.

How? (Grade 7)

Use research to see whether different market segments would prefer different products. Currently Ferrero's chocolate market share is booming in China and India thanks to their success targeting young children with Kinder Eggs.

So? (Grade 8)

It's very hard for new businesses to compete head-on with established giants such as Heinz or Cadbury. So it's cleverer to identify a small-ish segment that could be better served with a well-designed product. This enables the new business to establish itself – and gives a group of customers just what they want.

Grade 9

When a market is growing (think smartphones in 2014-2017) it's quite easy to find new ways to segment it. New opportunities open up. But it's much harder to segment a long-established market such as baked beans or bread; all the easy segmentation gaps have been filled. So lifestyle changes can be very important. In recent years, with the bread market in decline, '*Genius*' gluten-free bread has grown from nothing to £30 million of sales a year. Genius.

Do realise that segmentation has a downside: the smaller the target segment, the harder for sales revenues to cover all the costs of development, launch and production

---

Don't ignore lifestyle as a source of segmentation. It changes as fashions change, so it always throws up new business opportunities

---

Exam tip: don't allow segmentation to mush together with market mapping. Segmentation is about groups of people; mapping is about products (especially rival ones)

Market segmentation: 5-step logic chain (getting to the top response level)

Chain 1. Segmentation is a good way for a new business to find a market gap (1) … perhaps identifying that current shampoos aren't suited to Afro-Caribbean hair (2) so using demographic segmentation to identify a gap (3) … then design a product to meet the needs of customers in this segment (4) … allowing the product – at launch – to be priced a little higher than other shampoos. (5)

Chain 2. Because product life cycles come to an end, big companies need to keep launching new products; as the centre of the market may be crowded, segmentation may help (1) … perhaps in spotting that breakfast habits are different in cities than elsewhere. (2) This enabled Mondelez to spot the opportunity for its Belvita breakfast biscuit (3) … that families with an over-stretched lifestyle use as breakfast-on-the-go (4) …. allowing a chocolate and biscuit-maker to break into the breakfast market that used to be dominated by Kelloggs. (5)

Market mapping

What? (Grade 5 basics)

Market mapping uses a 2x2 grid to assess the strength of competition in different sectors of the market. Two key variables are identified that show the main factors affecting customer preferences. These often include price (high to low) and fashion (high to low). Then existing businesses or brands are placed on a grid showing these variables.

Why? (Grade 6)

Mapping can help identify gaps in the market. Years' ago high fashion meant high prices; Primark saw a gap for fashionable clothes at low prices; at the time, no-one was offering this. Mapping can also show where competitors are clustered; businesses such as Apple and Virgin rarely launch radical new products; they see where the market is clustered and try to do things better.

How? (Grade 7)

When entering a new market, research will be needed into customers' shopping habits and attitudes. This will probably require qualitative research into customer psychology. From this one can decide the two most-important variables affecting the market. Then finish off by plotting each competitor's position on the market map.

So? (Grade 8)

Most new products are stripped off the shelves within two years. They've flopped. So market mapping is an attempt to get an edge over rivals by finding more insights into where and why gaps exist – and where competition is toughest.

Grade 9

At the top level, you need to show that you understand the difference between mapping and segmentation. Mapping shows where your competitors sit on a grid based on variables such as the age of customers. Segmentation also considers the age of customers, but doesn't look at how much competition there is for each customer age group.

Do show you know the difference between mapping and segmentation. Segmentation is about the market; mapping is about the competition

Don't see mapping as a factual exercise, e.g. showing where each rival is located on a map. It's more a matter of marketing judgement, e.g. deciding whether to attack a market gap

Exam tip: market mapping is hard to explain, so it's hugely helpful to draw a grid and then explain it. Be careful to choose relevant factors, such as boy/girl in computer games software.

Market mapping: 5-step logic chain (necessary to get to the top response level)

Chain 1. A market map is a great help when thinking of starting a new business (1) ... as it identifies where competitors are clustered (2) ... and therefore where gaps may exist in the market (3). Identifying a market gap will help in persuading outside investors or lenders (4) ... that the business idea has a serious chance of becoming profitable – and perhaps can turn into something big. (5)

Chain 2. Existing companies can also benefit from – perhaps once a year – drawing up a detailed market map (1) ... which might identify changes from the previous year, such as a shift 'upmarket' by competitors (2). If rivals are tending to focus more on wealthier consumers who can afford higher prices it might be wise to follow this trend (3) ... but perhaps a new opportunity may open up at the lower-price end of the market (4) ... providing an opportunity for launching a new product or range of services targeted at the many families who are less well-off. (5)

Competitive Environment

What? (Grade 5 basics)

A measure of just how tough it is out there for a business to survive or even thrive. Currently it's extremely tough for toy and clothes shops because of the rise of internet retailers such as ASOS. In the high street competition is tough for restaurants because there are so many rivals – often right next door.

> **Do** be clear that market shares vary within what is usually a static market size. So a new success means existing companies are losing out.

Why? (Grade 6)

The competitive environment has become difficult because low interest rates have made it easier to borrow to start up a new business. So there are lots of new businesses starting up, and existing businesses can afford to expand.

How? (Grade 7)

How can businesses make sure they survive a fierce competitive environment? Of course they can't 'make sure'. But they can work harder to give customers what they want – in lower prices and better product design and quality. When competition is tough it's time to give customers better value and – especially – more smiles and more efficient service. Online goods must be delivered on time; and factors such as queue-times in shops must be checked carefully and minimised. Customers always matter – but just that bit more when competition is strong.

> **Don't** doubt the logic of the business world. If a poorly run business is closed down by the success of a brilliant newcomer, customers are better off.

So? (Grade 8)

In the exam, take care over phrases such as that the company 'operates in a fiercely competitive market'. Show that you recognise how tough this will be for the management in the business – and perhaps tougher still for staff. But as customers, we love a bargain price, we may even love a Closing Down Sale. The competitive environment pitches customer satisfaction against worker security.

Grade 9

For companies, more competitors means more pressure to keep costs down – which can be tough on staff, who may be pressed into signing job contracts that give them few rights – to pensions, say, or sick pay. But for consumers a fierce competitive environment means lots of special offers and fewer price rises. In effect, consumers get better value for money while employees find things a lot tougher.

> **Exam tip:** market mapping is a great way to build a picture of which company offers what to customers. It can help identify gaps, plus rivals' strengths and weaknesses

---

Competitive environment: 5-step logic chain (to get to the top response level)

Chain 1. If a business faces fierce competition it may need a tight focus on keeping costs down (1) ... especially costs that don't affect customers such as the size and location of Head Office (2) ... but it's also vital to work harder at details customers care about, such as on-time deliveries (3) ... which may require more management focus and therefore extra cost (4). Getting this balance right is essential for the business to survive and thrive. (5)

Chain 2. Some businesses have an easy life because they face little competition (1) ... such as Wrigley (95% of the UK market for gum) or Virgin Rail London-Manchester (100% share, i.e. no direct competition) (2). This usually leads to greedy pricing (3) ... and few new ideas on improving customer service (4) which shows that competition is valuable for customers (5)

Answering exams

Edexcel produces sample exam papers to help teachers. In these there is only one question directly about a competitive business environment. But in Edexcel's marking guidance there are far more references to competition. So it is a concept that can be used to answer many different questions.

Here are 3 questions where competition is a significant part of the answer:

P1 Q3d) Explain one disadvantage to a business of operating in a competitive business environment. (3 marks)

P1 Q7e) Evaluate whether Sally's business idea is likely to be a success. You should use the information provided as well as your knowledge of business. (12 marks)

P2 Q7d) In order to improve its competitive advantage, Argos has two options: Option 1: Lower prices or Option 2: Increase the speed of home delivery. Justify which one of these options Argos should choose. (9 marks)

On the right are strong answers to these three questions. They focus on using the competitive environment in the answers – so they are models for using this subject matter rather than models for how to score 9 or 12 marks.

For more on exam technique, see Section 3.

Grade 9 Answers (see questions on the left)

3d) *The more competitive the business environment the harder it would be to put prices up. So if a jump in raw material costs pushed up the total costs of the business, managers may be too worried about competitors to push their own prices up. This would cause profit per unit to decline.*

7e) *Sally's business idea is logical but limited. If there are not many personal trainers locally she should be able to build up a business from her position as a fitness instructor at the sports centre. But with one competitor charging £22 an hour and the other £20 (£220 / 11 sessions), she is taking a risk by charging £25 at the time of starting up. She is targeting a young market segment – who are likely to be highly price sensitive – so the price premium is odd.*

And in addition to the existing competition Sally should think about the potential for more rivals. Anyone can set up as a personal trainer without needing to invest much cash. So although it should be possible to break into this market, it may be very difficult to make much profit. It's too easy for new rivals to start up, keep prices down – and drain the profits away.

7d) *The text mentions that Argos has been struggling against the giant Amazon.com – on price and delivery. Some businesses face lots of competitors, which can be hard, but not as hard, perhaps, as facing up to a successful giant. If there were many, smaller rivals, option 1 would be attractive. You'd use the Argos buying power to keep costs down, then undercut the prices charged by rivals. But in this case the rival is Amazon – so Option 1 can be ruled out, because they'll always be able to cut prices *that* bit further.*

That leaves Option 2, which Argos should focus on. Amazon is super-efficient but Argos should be able to out-deliver Amazon if they focus on it 100%.

Aims and Objectives

What? (Grade 5 basics)

Business aims and objectives are the goals and targets that the owners wish to achieve. They can be divided into:

- financial targets such as survival, profit, sales, market share and financial security
- and non-financial targets such as social objectives, personal satisfaction, challenge, independence and control

Why? (Grade 6)

There are so many different pressures affecting a business at any one time that it's helpful if all staff know where the business is supposed to be heading. Managing a football team is easy: 3 points this Saturday please, and a trophy by May. Most businesses are much more complicated so clear aims and objectives provide a clear sense of direction which, in turn, helps in decision-making.

How? (Grade 7)

Anyone who starts their own business has personal objectives that may never be written down. A common non-financial one is to 'be your own boss'; at the start, most entrepreneurs are just looking for survival. Once things have settled down, the financial objectives will change towards market share and profit; still later there may be a change to financial security (perhaps by selling the business).

So? (Grade 8)

Different aims lead to different business decisions. A family-owned business aiming for long-term financial security (such as BMW) might invest for the future, taking care to avoid selling poor quality goods that might damage the brand/family name. Whereas a business aiming for maximum short-term profit might cut corners in order to boost this year's earnings. And a business started by an entrepreneur seeking 'a challenge' might take a few too many risks.

Grade 9

At the top level it's good to know the difference between aims and objectives. An aim is a general statement of where the business should be heading. An objective is much more specific, perhaps even SMART: Specific, Measurable, Achievable, Realistic, Time-bound. Aim: Profit Growth. Objective: boost profit by 25% this year and 50% within 3 years.

Do be clear that aims and objectives are the drivers of business decisions, e.g. deciding whether to launch a new product or to squeeze more profit out of existing ones.

Don't assume that businesses set the right objectives. Tesco once set the objective of more sales and ended up in a disastrous expansion into the USA. It cost £2 billion in losses.

Exam tip: examiners are particularly interested in social objectives, e.g. setting up a business with a social or charitable purpose. Even charities need some profits to fund their charity spending.

Aims and Objectives: 5-step logic chain (to get to the top response level)

Chain 1. Aims and objectives are at the heart of a start-up business plan (1) ... as they set out the targets for the first few years (2) ... perhaps including SMART targets (3) ... that show the precise profit target for Year 1 and the finance required to get there (4). Without clear aims and objectives it would be hard – perhaps impossible – to get any outsider to invest in your new business. (5)

Chain 2. Aims and objectives differ between businesses because they are based on circumstances, competition and individual preferences (1) ... so one business tries to maximise market share (think Samsung) while another wants long-term financial security (2) ... in order to hand over the business to the next generation (3) ... perhaps with a reputation for quality and integrity (4) to reflect well on the family name (5)

Answering exams

Aims and objectives will frequently be tested in the Paper 1 exam, and may also be an important part of Paper 2 answers. Here are 3 questions where aims and objectives are at the heart of things:

Q1. Explain one benefit to a business of having clear aims and objectives. (3 marks)

P2 Q7e) Evaluate whether Sainsbury's is likely to benefit from its takeover of Home Retail Group. You should use the information provided as well as your knowledge of business. (12 marks)

Q3. Discuss whether it is possible for a business to succeed if the owner/partners have different aims and objectives for the business. (6 marks)

On the right are strong answers to these three questions. They focus on how aims and objectives can be used in the answers – so they are models for using this topic rather than models for how to score 9 or 12 marks.

For more on exam technique see Section 3.

Extra Exam Tip:

Entrepreneurs often have a personal objective of 'being their own boss'. In fact running a small business can soon feel like you have many bosses, from customers to big, powerful suppliers. So be alert to when an owner's non-financial aims and objectives prove hard to achieve in reality.

Grade 9 Answers (see questions on the left)

Q1 *Clear aims and objectives matter when a business starts taking on extra staff. Everyone needs to know the targets the business has for the future. This makes it easier to make the right choice when staff are faced with tricky decisions.*

7e) *The answer depends a great deal on Sainsbury's aims and objectives. If they are trying to boost this year's profit it is unlikely to occur by buying up Argos. Takeovers often struggle in first months because employees and managers have to get used to new, different ways of working. Personal job satisfaction can be sacrificed as people try to overcome difficult problems.*

The financial benefits might shine through quite quickly, such as attracting higher sales as people buy through Sainsbury but pick up at Argos. Yet there may be pressures and frustrations that eat away at staff motivation, meaning that the financial benefits might disappear as weakening motivation starts to affect productivity.

Q3. *If one boss wants high profits while the other is focused on social objectives, the business has a problem. The two bosses will make different decisions when faced with similar problems or customer queries. That will be confusing for staff who won't know the 'right' thing to do when faced with a similar situation.*

Despite this, it must still be possible for the business to succeed if it's fortunate enough to be in the right place at the right time. The launch of Greene & Black's organic chocolate was full of problems between the two founders – yet Cadbury bought the business for £50 million. Surely that's success.

So although a failure to agree aims and objectives is a huge handicap, it is still possible for the business to be a success.

Business revenue and costs

What? (Grade 5 basics)

Revenue is the value of the sales made over a period of time, perhaps a month. It is calculated by multiplying Price x Quantity sold. So a chip shop selling 60 cod & chips at £6 each has made £360 of revenue.

Costs need to be broken down into two types: fixed and variable. Fixed costs are unaffected by the level of sales or output, e.g. rent and lighting. Variable costs vary as output varies, such as raw materials. The more crisps Walkers makes, the more potatoes they have to buy.

The formula for Total costs is: Fixed costs + (Variable cost per unit x Quantity). So if the chip shop uses £2 of fish and potatoes and has £150 per day of fixed costs, its total costs are: £150 + (£2 x 60 = £120) = £270 a day.

> **Do** take care to read calculation questions twice over. They 'only' amount to 10% of the marks, but that gives scope for good students to gain 2 grades on others.

Why? (Grade 6)

Breaking costs into fixed and variable can help in setting prices. Restaurants typically calculate their variable costs on a dish and then multiply by 4 to get the selling price. A piece of steak costing £5 would be priced at £20 to the customer. That should leave enough to cover the fixed costs and still make an overall profit.

How? (Grade 7)

Costs are broken into variable or fixed depending on how they are paid out. One employee may be paid a salary (same every month); this is a fixed cost. Another may be paid per item produced (piecework) or sold (commission); this is a variable cost.

> **Don't** muddle pence and pounds. If the examiner is using both, convert the pence to pounds and no mistakes can happen, e.g. 60p becomes £0.6.

So? (Grade 8)

Getting an accurate understanding of costs is important to a business, because it allows profits to be forecast: 'If we sell 3,000 of these, we'll make a £4,000 profit'. That, in turn, allows the business to plan how that £4,000 is to be spent, perhaps invested in improving the website.

Grade 9

The gap between revenue and costs can be widened if clever marketing or branding generates clear added value. The higher the added value the wider the gap – making it easier to generate high profits. Companies that show brilliance at added value, such as Apple and Chanel, often weave strong branding together with great design and great technology.

> **Exam tip**: take real care over the term 'fixed costs'. Fixed does **not** mean 'don't change' it means 'don't change as output changes'.

Revenue and costs: 5-step logic chain (needed to get to the top response level)

Chain 1. To cut costs a business can tackle variable and/or fixed costs (1) Fixed costs can be cut by making administrative staff redundant (2) … but that may lead to poor management and inefficiency (3) causing fixed and even variable costs to move up again (4) leaving total costs no lower than before (5).

Chain 2: To boost revenue a business must sell more items or manage to push the price up (1) without losing much sales volume (2). Selling more units is easy if consumer trends are with you (more gluten-free bread when consumers are focused on 'free-from' foods) (3) but hard when there's no growth in market size (4) perhaps forcing a business to revamp its packaging or find a new, better recipe for its product (5).

Worked examples (with answers)

Grade 5 question:

Q1. A company has weekly sales of 400 units at £12 each. Variable costs per unit are £3 and total fixed costs are £2,000 for the week.

Calculate a) Total revenue for the week and b) Total costs for the week.

ANSWER

1a) Total revenue = Price x Quantity

1a) Total revenue = £12 x 400 = £4,800

1a) Total costs = Fixed costs + Variable costs

Total costs = £2,000 + (£3 x 400) = £3,200

Grade 8/9 question:

Q2. An online fashion clothing site has monthly revenues of £12,000 from the sale of 240 items. It buys in the clothes for £10 per item and has total costs of £8,500.

Calculate:

2a) The fashion site's fixed costs per month

2b) The fashion site's average selling price per item.

ANSWER

2a) If total costs are £8,500 and total variable costs are £10 x 240 = £2,400, then fixed costs must be £8,500 - £2,400 = £6,100

2b) Total revenue divided by the number sold gives the average selling price.

So £12,000 / 240 items = £50 price per item

Business calculations (test yourself)

Grade 5 questions:

Q1. DF Ltd has monthly sales of 800 units, fixed costs of £1,500, variable costs of £2 per unit and a selling price of £8.

Calculate a) DF Ltd's monthly sales revenue and b) its total costs.

Q2. An airline sells 120 seats at £50 each and 80 at £90 each. The variable cost per passenger is £5 but the fixed costs per flight are £9,200.

Calculate a) the revenue per flight and b) the total costs per flight.

Grade 6/7 question:

Q3. A bakery sells 500 cakes a week at £2 each and 600 loaves of bread at £2.50 each. The bakery's total costs of £2,100 a week include variable costs of £1 per unit (cake or bread).

Calculate a) the weekly revenue and b) the weekly fixed costs.

Grade 8/9 question:

Q4. A surfing school charges £30 per one-hour lesson and pays its tutors £12. Last month the school's revenue was £15,000 and its total costs were £12,500 of which £5,000 were fixed.

Calculate a) The number of surfers taught last month (the sales volume) and b) The total variable costs per hour.

For answers see Section 3.6 (back of book)

Profit and Loss

What? (Grade 5 basics)

Profit is made when revenues are greater than costs. To calculate profit, use the formula: Profit = Revenue *minus* Total costs. If the costs are greater than the revenues the profit will be negative. That is known as a loss.

Profit is important for two reasons: it provides surplus capital that can be reinvested in the business to finance growth or to finance new equipment to help boost efficiency. In addition profit can be paid out to shareholders in the form of annual dividends.

For exercises to practise profit, see the right hand page.

> **Do** treat profit as a hugely important part of the long-term success of a business. Profits need to be high enough to finance the costs involved in keeping the business up to date

Why? (Grade 6)

Without profit few organisations would last long. Machinery and vehicles inevitably get older and more unreliable – so they need to be replaced. Profit can be used to pay for replacement costs such as this – enabling the business to stay up-to-date. Profit also provided finance for business expansion.

How? (Grade 7)

Profit stems from added value, in other words the ability to charge customers more than the cost of the materials used to make a product. The higher the gap between the selling price and the variable costs, the bigger the chance that fixed costs can be covered, leaving a surplus that is profit.

> **Don't** ever muddle revenue and profit. Oddly, students do it all the time. Revenue is just the money from sales. Profit is revenue minus costs.

So? (Grade 8)

If a business is making a loss, it is using more resources than it is creating in value to customers. So it acts as a drain on the economy. A profit-making business is not only making money for shareholders, it is also creating economic wealth for the community. Profit sometimes seems to be seen as a dirty word, implying that my profit is your loss. Generally, profit is an important and useful part of business.

Grade 9

Many exam questions revolve around boosting profits or overcoming losses. The logic is always the same: consider how best to boost revenues, taking care to think about the short-term and long-term issues. Then analyse how to cut costs without upsetting customers. Shrinking that chocolate bar seems a crazy way to do it, but finding a new, smaller, cheaper home for Head Office makes perfect sense.

> **Exam tip**: it helps you and the examiner if you start a profit calculation with a formula. Then follow it through (and the examiner can follow your logic)

Profit and Loss: 5-step logic chain (necessary to get to the top response level)

Chain 1. In the short-term cost-cutting is the surest way to boost profit (1) especially if you cut the things customers won't notice, such as staff job security (2) ... perhaps by replacing full-time jobs with temporary jobs for lower-wage students (3). But if motivation is undermined within your workforce there may be a fall in productivity (4) making costs start to creep up again in the longer term (5).

Chain 2: If a business is making regular losses a solution must be found before the cash is drained from the bank accounts (1). One answer is to investigate which part of the business is making the losses (2) ... and consider closing that down while refocusing efforts on the remaining business units (3). The remainder may actually be quite profitable (4) ... or may benefit from greater management involvement to ensure better decision-making and the avoidance of costly mistakes (5).

Worked examples (with answers)

Grade 5/6 question:

Q1. A company has weekly sales of 500 units at £12 each. Variable costs per unit are £4 and total fixed costs are £3,200 for the week.

Calculate profit or loss for the week

ANSWER

1. Profit = Revenue – Total costs

Revenue = Price x Quantity

Revenue = £12 x 500 = £6,000

Total costs = Fixed costs + Variable costs

Total costs = £3,200 + (£4 x 500) = £5,200

So profit = £800

Grade 8/9 question:

Q2. An egg producer has monthly revenues of £72,000 from the sale of 72,000 boxes. Its variable costs are 50p per box and fixed costs are £20,000 a month.

Calculate:

2a) The producer's monthly profit

2b) The profit if a sharp increase in demand causes sales to double.

ANSWER

2a) Profit = Revenue – Total costs

If total variable costs are 50p x 72,000 = £36,000, and fixed costs are £20,000, then total costs are £56,000

So profit = £72,000 - £56,000 = £16,000

Business calculations (test yourself)

Grade 5/6 questions:

Q1. BGT Ltd has weekly sales of 100 units at £25 each. Variable costs per unit are £10 and fixed costs are £900 for the week.

1a) Calculate profit or loss for the week

1b) Calculate profit or loss if sales double

Q2. An online clothes store sells 400 shirts at £15 each and 250 scarves at £4. The shirts cost £4 each from Bangladesh and the scarves £2 each. The business has weekly fixed costs of £1,200.

Calculate the weekly profit.

Grade 6/7 question:

Q3. A farmer sells £10,000 of strawberries a day at £2 a kilo. The variable production costs are 40p a kilo and fixed costs are £6,500.

Calculate a) the weekly total costs and b) the weekly profit.

Grade 8/9 question:

Q4. A surfing school charges £30 per one-hour lesson and pays its tutors £10. Last month the school's revenue was £24,000 and its total costs were £15,000 of which £7,000 were fixed.

Calculate:

a) The number of surfers taught last month (the sales volume)

b) The profit last month.

c) The profit next month, if sales rise by 50%.

For answers see Section 3.6 (back of book)

Break even

What? (Grade 5 basics)

The break-even level of output occurs when all costs are covered by revenues, leaving neither a profit nor a loss. There is a formula for calculating that point (see below) or it can be identified on a break-even chart. It's the level of output where the revenue line crosses the line for total costs. A break-even chart shows the level of profit at every possible level of output, from zero to the maximum production level.

Why? (Grade 6)

A break-even chart could help an entrepreneur decide whether to start a new business (is it realistic to get the sales volume needed to beat the break-even level of output?) and can help an existing manager make decisions such as whether or not to cut prices.

How? (Grade 7)

To calculate the break-even level of output:

Step 1: Calculate price *minus* variable costs per unit

Step 2: Divide fixed costs by the above total

e.g. If a business with fixed costs of £2,000 a week has a selling price of £40 a unit and variable costs of £15 a unit

Step 1: £40 - £15 = £25

Step 2: £2,000 / £25 = 800 units (the break-even level of output)

So? (Grade 8)

The real point of calculating break-even is to compare it with your actual sales level. The above example shows 800 as the weekly break-even level of output. That's fine if weekly sales are 2,000 units, as it means there's a healthy margin of safety. Sales can fall all the way from 2,000 units to 800 units before the business starts making losses. So the margin of safety is 1,200 units. But if sales are 900 units while the break-even level is 800, that's living on the edge.

Grade 9

Break-even gives an insight into the fundamentals of the business: is it profitable given the estimated future sales level? But it has a big weakness. It's only true at a point in time. It doesn't shows what's happening to sales (rising? Falling?) or trends in costs. Because it doesn't look ahead, it's not as useful as a cash flow forecast.

> **Do** remember how to measure profit on a break-even chart. It's the vertical distance between the revenue line and the total costs line

> **Don't** mistake the variable cost line for total costs. Remember that the variable cost line starts at £0 while total costs start where fixed costs start

> **Exam tip**: in the exam room, people often mix up break-even and the margin of safety. Remember, break-even is where the lines cross; and margin of safety is the gap between sales and break-even

---

Break even: 5-step logic chain (necessary to get to the top response level)

Chain 1. A break-even chart helps in making business decisions (1) because it shows the profit available at different levels of output (2) … perhaps helping a manager realise current sales are not enough, so new ideas are needed to boost demand (3). But if you rely too much on a break-even chart you might lose sight of cash flow (4) … which might be a big mistake, especially at the start of a business's life (5).

Chain 2: Calculating the break-even output is useful because it's more accurate than reading an answer off a graph (1) … which also allows a more accurate estimate of the margin of safety (2) … and therefore helps in evaluating how safe a position the business is in (3). A business wants its break-even point to be low (4) … and the margin of safety to be high (5).

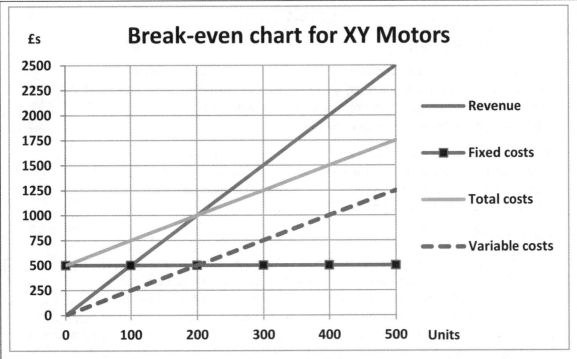

Break-even chart for XY Motors

Look at the above break-even chart and answer the following questions (answers bottom right).

1. What profit does the business make if it sells all 500 units?

2. What is its margin of safety if it sells all 500 units?

3. Calculate the business's variable costs per unit.

4. Explain what happens if the business can only sell 100 units.

5. What might cause an increase in the fixed costs for the business?

Further Questions (answers to the right)

Grade 5/6 question: Q6. Give two examples of factors that could cause variable costs to increase for a motor car manufacturer.

Grade 7/8 question: Q7. Identify two actions a business could take to reduce its break-even point.

Grade 8/9 question: Q8. Discuss the value of a break-even chart to a fast-growing business.

Business answers

1. £2,500 - £1,750 = £750.

2. 500 – 200 = 300 units

3. At 100 units the total variable cost is £250, so the variable cost per unit is £2.50

4. Total costs are £250 greater than total revenue, so it makes a loss of £250.

5. Increase in rents; increase in interest rates

6. An increase in supplier prices for components; an increase in raw material costs, e.g. the cost of sheet steel (steel to make the car's external panels)

7. Cut fixed costs, e.g. move Head Office to a cheaper location; or push the price up

8. Helps check profitability today, which may give confidence in future growth; but because the break-even chart looks at today only, it's not helpful for predicting the future.

Cash flow

What? (Grade 5 basics)

Cash flow measures the flows of cash in to – and out of – a firm's bank account. Cash inflows occur when customers pay up, when assets are sold off or when new capital is raised from outside lenders or investors. Cash outflows arise when suppliers are paid, when wages are paid and when loans are re-paid.

Net cash flow measures cash in minus cash out – perhaps over 24 hours or over a month. And when the cash out is greater than the cash in, 'negative cash flow' is occurring. Businesses often make a cash flow forecast to help anticipate when negative cash flows may cause a problem.

Why? (Grade 6)

Especially in the start-up phase, entrepreneurs are often told: 'cash is King'. Why? Because if you run out of cash – and can't pay suppliers or staff – the business will soon collapse. Your suppliers may even take you to court. So careful cash flow forecasting isn't an optional extra. It's always sensible business practice, but especially in the cash-hungry times: start-up and whenever there's rapid growth.

How? (Grade 7)

Cash is tough when you start because suppliers don't know you well enough to give you credit. So you have to pay cash up front – whereas your business customers expect credit periods of perhaps 2 or 3 months. So your cash inflow is weak at the start, while cash outflows are big.

So? (Grade 8)

To cope with the cash flow problem at start-up (for almost every new business), there is only one solution: raise enough capital at the beginning to give a generous cash cushion. That cushion will be eaten away in the early weeks, but hopefully be big enough to cover the period until customer payments start arriving.

Grade 9

Many students understand cash flow problems at start-up, but are less clear about the strains caused by growth. When sales are booming, lots of cash is needed to buy more stock, hire and train more staff and perhaps build more factory capacity. Yes, the cash inflows will eventually arrive from higher customer sales, but the strain on short-term cash flow can be very tough. So look for rapid growth as well as start-up as occasions when you must warn of potential cash flow difficulties.

> **Do** be practical about ways to improve cash flow. Few manufacturers can 'stop giving credit to customers' without causing customers to go elsewhere. Reduce credit periods, perhaps, but not cut completely

> **Don't** ever muddle cash flow and profit. Your examiner cares about the (quite subtle) difference. Cash flow is about the immediate effect on the bank account; profit is more long-term

> **Exam tip:** build your analysis of 6+ mark questions by breaking cash flow into cash inflow and cash outflow. Then show why inflows may be slowing and why outflows may be rising

---

Cash flow: 5-step logic chain (necessary to get to the top response level)

Chain 1. If monthly net cash flows are negative (1) the cash you started the month with will be lower at the month-end (2) ... and may even drag the bank account 'into the red' (3). This can only happen if the business has already agreed an overdraft with its bank (4) ... without an overdraft the bank will refuse to make any more payments – causing a serious cash flow crisis (5).

Chain 2. A boom in customer orders seems a reason to celebrate ... but the impact on cash can be tricky (1). You have to pay out more cash to suppliers, on staff overtime and perhaps to buy faster machinery (2) ... but the extra inflows from sales will take a few months to arrive (3). Until then, the business may operate with negative cash flow (4) ... causing the bank to lose confidence in you. (5)

Worked examples (with answers)

Grade 5/6 question:

Q1. A company's cash inflow this month is £7,000 and its outflow is £7,500. Its start-of-month opening balance was £3,000.

Calculate its end-of-month closing balance.

ANSWER

1. Month-end closing balance is:

Opening balance + monthly net cash flow

So £3,000 + (£500) = £2,500

Q2. Grade 6/7 question:

Calculate the answers to each of the missing numbers a) to e) in the table below.

	Jan	Feb	Mar
Opening balance	£1,200	£700	d)
Monthly cash in	£400	£800	e)
Monthly cash out	a)	£700	£900
Net cash flow	(£500)	b)	£200
Closing balance	£700	c)	£1,000

ANSWERS

2a) £900

2b) £100

2c) £800

2d) £800

2e) £1,100

Business calculations (test yourself)

Grade 5/6 questions:

Q1. BVK Ltd has cash outflow this month of £30,000 and a cash inflow of £33,000. Its end-of-month closing balance will be £10,000.

Calculate its start-of-month opening balance.

Grade 7 question

Q2a) A clothing business has an unexpected boom in orders in July, thanks to a celeb tweet that goes viral. Calculate the missing items within its cash flow.

	June	July	August
Opening balance	£3,000	£3,300	(£900)
Monthly cash in	£2,500	£2,800	£3,900
Monthly cash out	£2,200	c)	£6,900
Net cash flow	a)	(£4,200)	d)
Closing balance	b)	(£900)	e)

Q2b) Briefly explain how it is possible for a business to have a negative end-of-month closing balance. (3)

Grade 8/9 question:

Q3. Discuss why the cash flow forecast for a new pizza delivery business might prove to be incorrect. (6)

For answers see Section 3.6 (back of book)

Sources of business finance

What? (Grade 5 basics)

Businesses need a balance of long term and short term finance. When starting up, long term finance is needed to buy things needed in the long term. For a new factory it might be such as property, machinery and vehicles. For an online shop it might be warehousing, property for a head office and the cost of developing a fantastic e-commerce site. But short term finance is also needed, to pay suppliers for materials or stock, or to pay the day-to-day bills such as electricity and telephone.

Why? (Grade 6)

Short-term needs should be matched by short-term finance. When buying stock from suppliers, nothing is better than trade credit. And if the payments have to be made before customers pay their bills, an overdraft is a perfect way to finance needs that may be for just a day or two.

The same logic applies to long-term finance. Long term needs such as buying robotic machinery should not be financed from short term sources. Retained profit or a 5-year bank loan would be far more suitable.

How? (Grade 7)

Many of the sources of long-term finance come from outside the business and its founders. Venture capital, crowd funding and some share capital can only be raised by persuading outsiders to risk their cash. This requires either a compelling business story (such as *One Water*: 'all profits from our bottled water go to clean water projects in Africa') or a clear, convincing plan to make big profits. Socially beneficial projects work well with crowd funding, while most venture capital investors are willing to take big risks as long as there are huge potential profits.

So? (Grade 8)

Most entrepreneurs find that good ideas are easy to finance. Harder is to finance ideas that have little distinctiveness. Would you want to invest in a new business that will be the 7th men's hairdresser on a high street? Nor would anybody else. So the key to getting finance for start-up is to find a real business opportunity. And the key to finance when you've already started is to use retained profits as the main source.

Grade 9

When thinking of business finance, think of risk. The least risky sources are the owner's own capital and the company's own capital (its retained profits). The riskiest sources are:

- Financial risk from the cash flow strains caused by debt (loans and overdrafts)
- the risk of losing control that comes from selling shares – whether to ordinary shareholders or to venture capital providers.

Clever entrepreneurs find a careful balance between these two risks.

Do start by thinking about the capital need: short or long-term? Make sure to match short-term need to short-term capital – and so on

Don't follow the crazy logic of Dragon's Den, which makes it seem that obtaining finance is the clever/hard bit. Making a profit from trading – now *that's* hard.

Exam tip: avoid muddling bank loans with overdrafts. A bank loan is great for borrowing a single amount for several years; the flexibility of an overdraft makes it work for financing day-day business ups and downs.

Sources of finance: 5-step logic chain (to get to the top response level)

Chain 1. If you buy a lorry using your overdraft (1) … you'll find that high interest charges add up over the years (2) … and by using up the overdraft you may run out of credit to help you get through tough times of year (3) … such as the lead-up to Christmas for '*Festive*' – the UK's largest producer of tinsel (4). Retailers such as John Lewis expect deliveries in October but pay in January, so an overdraft is needed to make up for the Autumn cash-flow shortfall. (5)

Chain 2. Crowd funding works brilliantly for products that customers are attracted to (1) … such as a new range of UK-produced, organic petfood (2). The customers' enthusiasm makes them happy to invest sums such as £100 to help get the business going. (3) But there are lots of valuable business ideas that aren't that attractive, such as an online cleaning service for work uniforms (4) … so crowd funding isn't effective in all circumstances. (5)

Answering exams

Edexcel produces sample exam papers to help teachers. In these there is only one question directly about sources of finance. But in Edexcel's marking guidance there are plenty of mentions of sources of finance. So it is an area that helps in answering many different questions.

Here are 3 questions where competition is a significant part of the answer:

P1 Q3c) Explain one possible conflict that can exist between stakeholders of a business. (3 marks)

P1 Q5c) Analyse the impact on *Meringue* of using a bank loan to pay for the contactless payment system. (6 marks)

P1 Q7d) Sally is considering whether or not to buy a franchise to start up on her own. Justify whether or not Sally should buy a franchise. (9 marks)

On the right are strong answers to these three questions. They focus on how sources of finance can be used in the answers. They are models for using finance rather than models for how to score 9 or 12 marks.

Grade 9 Answers (see questions on the left)

3c) *Business managers may want to invest in the business's future while shareholders want higher dividend payouts, i.e. less capital retained in the business in the form of reinvested profits. This conflict is likely to be resolved in favour of shareholders as they own the business.*

5c) *A contactless payment system will be needed over several years, therefore a bank loan is a good medium-long term method of finance. But although the text mentions the raid growth in sales revenue, there is nothing about the level of profits. If Meringue is barely profitable, a bank loan would be a source of concern. Loans drain cash flow in two ways: monthly outflows (interest payments) and then of course the capital must be repaid. The owners should think carefully about whether they can afford the contactless payment system if they have no retained profits to finance it.*

7d) *The text says that Sally has saved enough capital to finance her start up – which is a fantastic situation. But it's not clear whether that includes the cost of buying into a franchise operation. After all, these can easily cost £100,000. If the high cost forces her to need outside financing such as a bank loan, this might be an important reason to avoid that route. Better, perhaps, to be self-funded with an independent business than have a franchise funded by debt.*

Options for Start-up

What? (Grade 5 basics)

There are two types of business: those with limited liability and those with unlimited liability. If an entrepreneur hires a market stall and starts trading, this type of business is called a 'sole trader' and it has unlimited liability. This means any losses or debts created by the business remain the personal responsibility of the owner – that entrepreneur. Only by forming a company do the shareholder/owners enjoy limited liability.

Why? (Grade 6)

The reason 'limited liability' was introduced in the UK was to encourage entrepreneurs by reducing the risks to themselves and their families. You can invest your life savings – and potentially lose every penny – but with limited liability you can't be liable for any more than the sum you've invested. So banks can't come after your own money, or house, or car. With <u>un</u>limited liability they can.

How? (Grade 7)

To get the protection of limited liability you form a company. If Ian Marcouse forms Ian Marcouse Ltd (Ltd shows it's a private limited company), even if the company loses £500,000 the individual isn't liable. To form a company you need nothing more than proof of identity and to pay a fee of around £60.

So? (Grade 8)

The owners of unlimited liability businesses such as sole traders and partnerships must be extra careful to avoid losses. This may mean they hardly ever go on holiday, because they are too worried about leaving the business in a stranger's hands. The sole trader is unlimitedly liable, so a mistake made by friend trying to look after the business could lose the entrepreneur a fortune.

Grade 9

By law, every limited liability business must announce its status by showing Ltd or Plc (Public limited liability) after the company name. This warns others of the risks in dealing with a company. Perhaps the business will close down after running out of cash - and because the owners have limited liability, they don't need to pay the debts.

So it's riskier to lend money to a limited company than to an unlimited business.

Do decide on your business organisation early on in the process. A private company suits a small family business with a relatively high risk business idea

Don't refer to a franchise as a form of business ownership. A local franchise can be run as a limited or unlimited liability business. The franchise is just the method used to create customer appeal

Exam tip: look to see if the business name has Ltd or Plc after it. If not, the business has unlimited liability. And therefore is a big risk for the proprietor.

Options for start-up: 5-step logic chain (to get to the top response level)

Chain 1. Most new UK businesses start up as sole traders or partnerships (1) … meaning that they have unlimited liability (2) … this seems unnecessarily risky (3) … but it may be that the financial risks are too low to worry about (4) … such as starting a new online business in which failure would mean a waste of man-hours, but little risk of serious financial losses (5)

Chain 2. For a new business with serious growth prospects a private limited company structure is ideal (1) … because it's easy to bring new investors in by selling them shares in the business (2) … with no risk of further losses if the business fails (3). But the disadvantage is sharing future profits with your new shareholders (4) … who may also want a say in the main business decisions to be taken by the founder (5)

Answering exams

Of all the topics on the course, none is examined as regularly as this. I can virtually guarantee one or more direct questions on limited/unlimited liability or sole trader/partnership/private limited companies. Options for start-up can also be used to analyse many business situations and answer many high-mark questions, such as Q2c on the Edexcel specimen paper (see www.edexcel.com)

Here are three questions in which the options for start-up can be a significant part of the answer. The first two are based on Edexcel's specimen papers.

P1 Q1 (d) Explain one disadvantage to a sole trader of having unlimited liability. (3 marks)

P1 Q2 (c) Analyse the impact on *Meringue* of using a bank loan to pay for the contactless payment system (6 marks)

Q3. Discuss whether a new business would be better off starting out as a sole trader or a partnership. (6 marks)

On the right are strong answers to these three questions. They show the importance of understanding options for start up – and also show the need to have thorough understanding of every aspect of this topic.

With some topics it's possible that there will be no questions on *your* exam. Not in this case. Options for start-up will be there.

For more on exam technique see Section 3.

Grade 9 Answers (see questions on the left)

Q1. *For a sole trader the business is legally no different from the person. Personal liability is unlimited. So if the business loses money, its debts must be repaid by the individual owner.*

Q2 c) In the text Meringue is mentioned several times, but never with 'Ltd' to follow. As it's a legal requirement to 'own up' to limited liability, I conclude that Meringue is an unlimited liability organisation – probably a partnership.

Therefore taking out a bank loan to finance expansion doesn't just affect Meringue, it acts as a threat to the owners' personal finances. Bank loans cause two drains on cash flow: the regular monthly interest charges and the eventual cash repayment. If the business cannot afford to repay, Neil and Sue might end up losing their house.

Q3) The great strength of a sole trader is the clarity that one person is in charge – and that same person takes 100% of the profits – and 100% of any losses. On the other hand it's tough to get away on holiday, because it's hard to trust any 'business babysitter' when any mistake affects the unlimited liability of the sole trader.

A partnership has benefits, both by expanding the possible investment of capital (2+ investors rather than one) and by sharing responsibility. Going on holiday shouldn't be a problem. But entrepreneurs typically love to be in control – it's one of the great appeals of starting on your own – so it's very hard to share decision making. The risk is of arguments and disagreements that may tear the business apart.

On balance, it's only sensible to go into partnership if you know the partner well enough to be able to argue – scream, even – but still be on speaking terms tomorrow.

Franchising

What? (Grade 5 basics)

Franchising allows a small business to buy the rights to use the name, logo and trading method of an existing, successful company. Subway is one of the world's biggest examples, with nearly 50,000 Subway franchises worldwide. The huge advantage of buying into a franchise is that it can give your business instant customer appeal and recognition. The big downside is the cost. Subway's £10,000 starter fee is only the beginning of many charges, including paying out 12.5% of all the revenue your shop takes.

> **Do** think hard about whether buying into an established franchise is right for the individual described – and their personal business objectives

Why? (Grade 6)

The brand recognition provided by a strong franchise helps the entrepreneur raise capital in the first place. Banks are happier lending to someone buying into a successful franchise chain than one starting their own business from scratch. Also brand recognition helps bring customers in from Day 1; with a new independent business it might take weeks or months to build up a satisfactory level of sales.

How? (Grade 7)

To buy in to a franchise you approach the franchise owner and ask whether they have opportunities in the area you want to target. They may not; they may already have sold the rights to franchises in, say, Coventry. But if you are lucky you may get what you want. For a Subway franchise, their website is an important starting point: https://subwayfranchising.com/en-gb/. The website shows that starting a medium-sized Subway will cost around £150,000 – just to get it open.

> **Don't** ignore the risks involved in franchising. They may be lower than when opening something new and innovative, but no business is risk-free

So? (Grade 8)

Whether to start up with a franchise or to go independent is a classic business question. For a first-time entrepreneur a franchise makes sense because lots of the business thinking is done for you. So you are running a business using the methods laid down by the franchise owner. Not quite 'being your own boss'.

Grade 9

Students are inclined to underestimate the risks in opening a franchise. The risk is not that it will be a disaster; rather more that it may be a bit of a trap, with the entrepreneur finding that the franchise fees drain the business of meaningful profits. And the franchise rules of operation make it frustrating to run.

> **Exam tip:** help the examiner by distinguishing clearly between the franchise owner (e.g. Subway Inc of America) and the entrepreneur buying the local franchise

---

Franchising: 5-step logic chain (to get to the top level of response)

Chain 1. Buying a franchise makes sense for a first-time entrepreneur (1) … or for one who needs to minimise the risk of outright financial failure (2) because franchises are already proven to meet customer needs (3) … and have established methods of operation that make it hard to fail. (4) But high start-up costs and ongoing fees make it hard to make big profits out of a franchise. (5)

Chain 2. For an entrepreneur who wants independence and control, a franchise could be a big mistake (1) … robbing the owner of creative opportunities such as marketing because that's handled centrally (2) … and often being too inflexible to allow local pricing decisions to be made. (3) The local franchise owner ends up managing people and finance, but not marketing or operations (4) Fortunately, despite some frustrations, this is a relatively low risk way to start a business career. (5)

Business Location

What? (Grade 5 basics)

In business, location can be a hugely important factor: think of the busy sweetshop near a station or the hamburger stall outside Wembley stadium. Important factors influencing location are nearness ('proximity') to the market, labour, materials and competitors. Now there's another huge influence: the internet in general and e-commerce in particular.

Do think about the circumstances of the business being looked at: e-commerce or physical; service or production; needing a high-skill workforce or a low-cost one?

Why? (Grade 6)

Before the internet there were two main factors in location: direct convenience, as in having a coffee shop two doors from your work; and the alternative convenience from jumping in the car and driving to the nearest shopping centre, Now e-commerce threatens the second of these. As I'm writing this Toys R Us is closing a third of its UK branches – just to survive. Why go to a big self-service shed when you can buy on Amazon in a few clicks – and probably at a lower price?

How? (Grade 7)

To make a location decision a business must weigh up the potential revenues versus the costs at a range of possible locations. The rent on a shop in the main part of the high street might be 4 times higher than in a side street; but if there are 5 times more passers-by, it might be a price worth paying. If you're selling impulse-purchase goods such as Krispy Kreme doughnuts, it's wise to go for the high price/high passers-by site. If the products are a planned purchase such as a carpet, customers will find you when they need you – so stick to the side street.

Don't ignore the costs involved in a good location. High revenues are no use if costs are even higher. Profit is the best way of judging one location v. another

So? (Grade 8)

Entrepreneurs with limited start-up capital are tempted to buy into a low-rental location. They think of the relatively low break-even position for the business and see it as the lower-risk decision. But you can't expect people to go out of their way for an impulse purchase. So a 'low-risk' option may be the riskiest of all.

Grade 9

Choosing the right location is a huge issue for a physical retailer, but unimportant to an online business. When you buy from ASOS you have no idea where the business is located (nor do you care). So ASOS can find a low-cost location where all that matters is getting the right staff and being close to good transport links. As the world moves more towards e-commerce, this pattern will increase – perhaps leading to falls in the rental values at shopping centres and in the high street.

Exam tip: boost your marks by breaking location costs down into fixed and variable. Locating in Wales may mean low property (fixed) costs, but higher transport (variable) costs

---

Business location: 5-step logic chain (to get to the top level of response)

Chain 1. For a retail ice cream shop, physical location is critical (1) ... because lots of ice creams are bought on impulse (2). So even though the rental cost may be high (3) ... the higher customer numbers should more than pay for that (4) allowing the profits made in the summer to be high enough to get the business through the winter (5)

Chain 2. An ice cream factory can be located where there's the right mix of staffing and costs (1) ... with refrigeration there's no need to be in a town centre, so costs can be kept down. (2) Fixed costs such as property and salary bills can push the break-even point too high (3) ... so it's better to find a low-cost location (4)... and put more cost into higher-quality ingredients to make better ice cream (5)

Introduction to the Marketing Mix

What? (Grade 5 basics)

The marketing mix is the way a business uses 4 factors to turn its marketing ideas into a clear plan. The four are product, price, promotion and place; so the marketing mix is often called the '4Ps'. A successful mix is one that achieves the marketing objectives of the business, such as to build market share or to outsell a rival.

Why? (Grade 6)

The importance of the mix is that the 4 factors have to be coordinated with care. In other words it's no good having glossy advertisements in Vogue and the Sunday Times if you're going to promote your product by shouting Buy One Get One Free! The image and the reality will clash (what if Mercedes promoted its cars with Buy One Get One Free??).

How? (Grade 7)

The starting point is to decide where to target your product (at a niche market perhaps?). Then:

- design the right Product to meet the needs and wants of that type of customer
- set the Price that matches those customers' expectations and incomes
- Promote the product in the right way (social media for a younger niche; TV for an older target market)
- then find the best way to Place your product in the right distribution channels to make it easy for customers to purchase

So? (Grade 8)

Getting the mix right is partly down to a good marketing team and partly down to the competitive environment. For many years Next plc seemed to be doing brilliantly in the clothing market; with hindsight its success was a lot to do with the failings of its main rival: Marks & Spencer. Your business might want to set high prices for its product, but if a close rival is setting lower prices, you may have to keep prices down. Decisions on the marketing mix need to bear in mind the competitive environment.

Grade 9

Getting the right, balanced marketing mix is hard. Even harder is successfully keeping up with changes in the marketplace. The competitive environment may be transformed by an Uber-type of new competitor. Or customer needs may change, as in 2018 when the demand for diesel cars fell sharply, with a clear switch to electric. No less important has been the impact of technology, with some traditional businesses being slow to switch to digital communication (advertising through social media) and to e-commerce.

Do focus on the need for the 4Ps to fit together and work together. And be willing to speak out if a business has one 'P' out of line from the other three.

Don't make this part of business seem easy. Businesses as big as Mars and Toyota have struggled to find the right mix in the new high-tech, online era.

Exam tip: remember that there's a much more detailed look at the marketing mix in Theme 2. Questions can come up on the '4Ps' or on any individual one of them.

The marketing mix: 5-step logic chain (to get to the top response level)

Chain 1. A successful marketing mix needs the 4Ps to work well together (1) … based on understanding and meeting customer needs (2) … so that the price charged seems right for the product on offer (3) ... and the methods of promotion reach the right people in a way that takes them from product awareness to product purchase (4) … with the distribution methods making it easy for people to buy what they want when they want. (5)

Chain 2. A service business needs a different mix from a producer (1) … often based on providing a more individualised 'product' (2) .., such as Starbucks with its amazing range of choice (3). Other mix factors matter, such as promoting the brand name and the idea of service and variety (4) backed by store locations placed for customer convenience and a price people are willing to pay (5).

Answering exams

Edexcel produces sample exam papers to help teachers. In these there are several questions about the marketing mix. There are also broader questions in which a paragraph on the '4Ps would be very useful. Here are two questions set by the exam board:

P1 Q4a) Outline one method of promotion that would be appropriate for *Meringue*. (2 marks)

P1 Q6d) Neil and Sue are considering two options to reduce the amount they need to sell to break even.

Option 1: Increasing average prices by 10%

Option 2: Reducing the cost of ingredients by using a cheaper supplier.

Justify which one of these two options Neil and Sue should choose. (9 marks)

For more on exam technique see Section 3.

Grade 9 Answers (Qs. on the left)

4a) As there's 'lots of passing trade' a valuable method of promotion would be to establish a stunning window display of the 'high quality bread and pastries. That should attract people to stop, come in and buy.

6d) *Option 1 suggests a 10% price rise. But this has been put forward in isolation – ignoring the other aspects of the marketing mix. Although Meringue's 'place' is ideal – with lots of passing trade – a glance at the photo shows a pretty basic sandwich bar: not a shop that can easily support sharp price rises. While at this location it would be hard to justify a price rise.*

And then there's Option 2, which threatens to reduce the quality reputation for product by focusing on getting a cheaper supplier. This, in turn, could threaten the long-term position of the business. If products are 'high quality' one minute, it's risky to undercut that by buying more cheaply unless you're certain that the actual quality of the ingredients in unchanged.

Further Exam tip. As the 9-mark question is always Option 1 versus Option 2, expect the '4Ps' of the marketing mix to feature quite regularly. Along the lines of: 'Should XYZ Ltd focus mainly on Price or Promotion when launching its new product? Justify your answer.' A different pairing of mix factors will generate several exam questions over the years.

Business plans

What? (Grade 5 basics)

First-time entrepreneurs face a struggle to bring together all the financial, marketing, production and human aspects of running a business. A business plan is a way to cope with this problem. It's a document that sets out the business aims and objectives plus all the financial and other plans for how to achieve them.

Why? (Grade 6)

For new and experienced entrepreneurs alike, a business plan is a valuable document for gaining external finance. Bankers want to see your plan to help them judge the risks involved in the business proposition. While for banks the key thing is risk, for potential investors in the company's shares, at least as important are the potential rewards. Venture capital investors are looking for 'scalability' – the ability of the small business idea to be expanded into something huge – and hugely profitable.

Do show the examiner you understand how difficult business planning must be for a first-time entrepreneur. The more knowledge and experience of the industry, the better the chances of success

How? (Grade 7)

Writing a business plan starts with the opportunity you have identified. Perhaps your town has only one, pricey but second-rate, Thai restaurant. And you're sure you can do better. Then you need some market research, a forecast of weekly revenues and – most important of all – a cash flow forecast. Other decisions can then be added in such as the planned location, the planned marketing mix and the desired sources of finance.

Don't focus too much on profit in the early stages of a new business. Cash is King.

So? (Grade 8)

Any entrepreneur who seeks outside investors or lenders needs a business plan. But they may find the plan far more useful still. Once funding is sorted and it's time for action, the business plan helps provide a week-by-week guide for what to do, how to do it and the maximum that can be spent. For first-time entrepreneurs especially, the plan can become their business bible.

Grade 9

The secret to success with a business plan is to be doubly careful: to estimate your revenues and cash inflows on the low side, and cash outflows on the high side. And then show even more caution by making a generous allowance for 'contingencies' - things that shouldn't go wrong, but might. Bankers will be particularly impressed by a plan that shows understanding that starting a business is hard – so plenty of spare cash should be built into the plan.

Exam tip: for a 6, 9 or 12-mark question, focus your answer on the key parts of the business plan: the idea, the market research and the cash flow forecast. Don't end up listing lots of different elements of the plan.

Business plans: 5-step logic chain (getting to the top response level)

Chain 1. For a young, first-time entrepreneur bankers and investors will pick holes in the plan (1) … so it will need to be exceptionally well researched (2) … especially in the forecasts of sales and cash flow (3). It would help to have the plan checked thoroughly by an older mentor (4) ... who could come along to meetings with bankers and investors – to reassure them that the idea has legs. (5)

Chain 2. If an entrepreneur has already succeeded with Shop Number 1, it's tempting to rush the business plan for shop 2 (1) … but actually there's a great opportunity here (2) ... a careful plan for Shop 2 would analyse why Shop 1 succeeded (3) … and how its success can be reproduced (4). This might encourage investors to put a lot of capital into the business, to finance rapid growth. (5)

Answering exams

Edexcel produces sample exam papers to help teachers. In these there is only one question directly about business plans. But in Edexcel's marking guidance there are plenty of mentions of business plans, or elements within the plan. So it is an area that helps in answering many different questions.

Here are 3 questions where business plans are a significant part of the answer:

P1 Q2e) Explain one reason why an entrepreneur would produce a business plan. (3 marks)

P1 Q3e) Discuss what a small business owner should consider when deciding upon the location for their business. (6 marks)

Q3. Sonia plans open her first business – a restaurant – financed entirely through her savings. She is still working full-time and wondering whether to do a business plan. Justify whether or not she should spend time writing a business plan. (9 marks)

On the right are strong answers to these three questions. They focus on how a business plan can be used in the answers. They are models for using the plan rather than models for how to score 6 or 9 marks.

For more on exam technique see Section 3.

Grade 9 Answers (see questions on the left)

3c) One reason is if the entrepreneur is hoping to take out a bank loan. The bank wants evidence that their capital is safe because the business plan is well-researched and the cash flows estimated with caution.

5c) When choosing a location the small business owner should think about the whole business plan. If the opportunity is to provide a dry cleaning service to busy commuters, a location right by the train station would be perfect – perhaps essential. A side-street location may have a much lower rent, but busy commuters won't make a detour, so the business may never reach its break-even point.

On the other hand there may be a risk in following the business plan too rigidly. The plan may refer to a city-centre location, but if premises become free at a busy, out-of-town shopping mall, it may be wise to quickly rethink – and seize the opportunity. In business, great locations don't come up that often.

3. Most business plans are produced for external funders such as banks or venture capital investors. Clearly that's not needed in this case. But Sonia needs to be aware that all new businesses have a significant risk of failure – and restaurants are among the riskiest. So she should focus on how *she* might benefit from doing a business plan. Simply doing a plan will help her think through all that has to be done – and in what order. And that might reduce the risk of her making mistakes that cause the business to fail.

On the other hand she might get too caught up in a detailed plan that is too rigid to be helpful in the reality of business start-up. There will be lots of decisions that have to be made along the way – and a rigid plan might get in the way of intelligent decisions based on unexpected problems.

Stakeholders

What? (Grade 5 basics)

Stakeholders are the groups that have an interest in the success or failure of a business. Some rely on the business to make a living, such as suppliers, employees, managers and shareholders. Others rely on it to make life more or less pleasant or convenient, such as the local community, pressure groups, customers and the government.

Why? (Grade 6)

Businesses are at the heart of our economy and society. The decisions they make can generate high-paying jobs and wealth, or can treat customers or staff with contempt. Encouraging business leaders to think of all their stakeholders may help bring about decisions that are fairer to weak and strong alike.

How? (Grade 7)

Business decisions must always reflect the profit to be made. But business leaders could take greater account of what is fair to stakeholders. Partly because that's morally right, but also in the best long-term interests of the business. Staff that are fairly treated are more likely to stay – and more likely to work hard to help the business prosper.

So? (Grade 8)

Big businesses with a focus on long-term success will think about the best interests of stakeholders – and may even bring the stakeholders into the planning process. Customers, suppliers and workers are all likely to have valuable thoughts about how to make the business better and more successful. Who understands a school better than the teachers and the students? Talking to key stakeholders can be a huge step forward.

Grade 9

But it's wrong to think that all business leaders think this way. Many feel too much pressure on their shoulders to think what's best for the long-term future. They are trying to cope with today. So they concentrate on what the shareholders want. And what they usually want is a clear sign that profits are rising. This makes it vital to show that profit <u>now</u> is higher than profit 6 or 12 months' ago. So instead of thinking about all the stakeholders, decisions end up being made for short-term profit.

> **Do** consider the effect of a business on its stakeholders, plus the ways in which the stakeholders may affect the business. They may pressurise the business to change its ways of working

> **Don't** try to cover all the stakeholders when answering a 9 or 12-mark question. Pick two stakeholders that are important to the specific business

> **Exam tip:** many answers can be based on stakeholders v shareholders. In some cases leaders focus only on shareholders (and therefore profit) while others think about all the stakeholders

---

Stakeholders: 5-step logic chain (to get to the top level of response)

Chain 1. When businesses start up, they have to focus on cash flow and profit (1) … because if the business doesn't survive, no-one can benefit from it (2). But once the business is established and profitable decisions can take stakeholders into account (3) … such as checking on whether suppliers are looking after their staff properly (4) or giving your own staff a more enjoyable, social workplace – perhaps including buying the first round of drinks for all staff every Friday night. (5)

Chain 2. Private limited companies can grow to become quite large (1) … with family shareholders who may care a lot about the annual profit being made. (2) The business leader may feel pressured to make decisions based on the highest profits possible (3) … but that may weaken long-term customer or employee loyalty (4) … undermining the long-term growth prospects of the business. (5)

Answering exams

Edexcel produces sample exam papers to help teachers. In these there are several questions about stakeholders. There are also times when stakeholders can be used to help answer a broader question, perhaps about business objectives. So it is a concept that can be used to answer many different questions.

Here are 3 questions where stakeholders are a significant part of the answer:

1. Which one of the following best defines the term stakeholder? Select one answer. (1)

A An owner of a private limited company

B Someone with an interest in the success of a business

C Any individual who takes decisions within a business

D An individual who owns shares in a business

2. Explain one possible conflict that can exist between stakeholders of a business. (3)

3. *Zoella Beauty* is considering two options to develop the marketing mix of its beauty product line:

Option 1: Increase promotion of the brand.

Option 2: Reduce prices to compete with rival products.

Justify which one of these two options *Zoella Beauty* should choose. (9)

On the right are strong answers to these three questions.

For more on exam technique, see Section 3.

Grade 9 Answers (see questions on the left)

Q1. B.

Q2. *One conflict could be about productivity. Managers and owners always want to see efficiency increase. But if the market is in decline producing more units per worker will mean fewer workers are needed. So workers will fear job losses.*

Q3. Zoella Beauty is a brand based around the personality of vlogger Zoella, so promotion is a far better option than price cutting. Promotion can help build Zoella's reputation further, perhaps bringing more people in to watch her vlog. For Zoella, her followers and customers will be one and the same, so she probably sees them as 'hers', i.e. sees them quite personally. Clever promotion could help build on the stakeholder link between her and her customers.

However, a downside of promotion is that it actually costs money (whereas price cutting involves no cash outlay). If Zoella has too little cash to fund, shall we say, a TV advertising campaign, she might ask her suppliers to make a contribution. After all, they are stakeholders in her business who stand to gain considerably if she can generate higher sales.

In conclusion, promotion would be a better way to build the Zoella brand than price cutting, as long as she can find a way to finance her promotion strategy.

Technology and Business

What? (Grade 5 basics)

Changes in technology have always been important to business, such as the arrival of television, which in turn gave rise to powerful, nationwide advertising. But technology has rarely been as important as in the past 10-15 years with the arrival of digital technologies such as the internet. This has given rise to different types of technology such as e-commerce, social media, digital communication (including 'm-commerce' based on the power of modern smartphones) and digital payment systems such as Paypal.

Do think about the positives from technology – the opportunities for exciting new products. People focus too much on potential job losses

Why? (Grade 6)

Technology matters mainly because it brings about change. For many years ToysRUs was a hugely profitable star of U.S. toy retailing. Amazon changed all that by its online offer of low prices and home delivery. The change in technology created an opportunity for a new competitor.

How? (Grade 7)

How technology creates change is all-important. It does it by altering the factors that have created stability in the past. For over sixty years London 'Black cab' taxis offered a superior service based on the drivers' knowledge of the geography of London. The cabs were protected by regulations that prevented others from picking up customers on the street. The new technologies of GPS, online payments and the Uber 'App' changed all that.

Don't reduce technology just to the digital world of e-tailing.. Remember that automation and robotics are also a key part of modern business

So? (Grade 8)

All businesses need to be alert to new technologies and act sooner rather than later. Better to invest now and make a few mistakes than to invest too late and find you've been left behind. To do this successfully, it's important to hire bright young technologists who can spot opportunities for keeping ahead.

Grade 9

Grade 9 answers need to focus first on the effects of new technology on businesses. Slowness to respond might lead to falling revenues or a failure to benefit from falling costs. Beyond these effects there are important possible effects on the economy generally. Increased use of robots and AI (artificial intelligence) might cause unemployment; and might increase the gap between rich and poor. But the starting point is the effect on firms.

Exam tip: think about the specific business featured in the exam question. Some products and services will be dominated by new technology; others won't, for example hairdressing

---

Technology and Business: 5-step logic chain (to get to the top response level)

Chain 1. Technology can create repeatedly short product life cycles (1) ... as in the case of smartphones (2). This forces producers to invest heavily and constantly (3) ... to keep coming up with new product ideas (4) ... that can defeat competitors in the fight for market share. (5)

Chain 2. Used intelligently, modern digital technology gives scope to boost revenues *and* cut costs (1). Revenues might be boosted by effective marketing through social media (2) ... and costs cut by automated systems that cut labour costs (3). By squeezing costs down at the same time revenues are rising, profits can rise sharply (4) ... providing the capital for continuing investment as newer technologies come along (1).

Answering exams

It would be wise to expect regular exam questions on the impact of technology on business. Direct questions will turn up in Paper 1, but the impact of technology may also be an important factor in answering questions on Paper 2. Here are two possible exam questions; possible answers are on the right.

Q1. Explain **one** problem a small shop may have when bringing in new technology to turn itself into an online retailer. (3 marks)

Q2. Evaluate how new technology may influence the business activities of a small pizza delivery business. (12 marks)

On the right are strong answers to these two questions. They focus on how technology can be used in the answers – and Q2. can be regarded as a high-mark answer to a 12 mark question.

For more on exam technique see Section 3.

Grade 9 Answers (Qs. on the left)

1. 'Bringing in' technology understates the costs involved. They include buying the new equipment, including perhaps a professionally-designed e-commerce website. So one problem will be financing this change. If the business has been highly profitable – and has retained the profits – there should be no problem. But the decision to switch to online suggests profits haven't been great – so the financing may be difficult.

2. Technology could have a huge effect on the sales revenues of a pizza delivery business. Many modern customers expect to order their pizza through a mobile phone App; without offering this, the small business will steadily lose out to giants such as Domino's. Even if the small business provides a better pizza, convenience of ordering will sway a lot of customers. To survive in the long term, the small pizza business has to provide convenient ordering (which is why many opt for Just-Eat, which provides the technology for a fee).

Technology can also affect costs, such as labour costs. GPS mapping of delivery routes could help drivers be more efficient and therefore make more deliveries per shift. That in turn will reduce the delivery cost per customer order – cutting total costs. With improved revenues and lower costs, technology could transform profits.

Further Exam tip. Do you know much about technology in factories? Probably not. Take a look at this clip of a robot installing a windscreen on a car production line. This is a job that used to take 4 people 6 minutes. This robot takes 90 seconds. See: https://www.youtube.com/watch?v=k2M66I7YdCE (if this doesn't work, simply Google 'robot windscreen installation' and a new version of the clip will come up).
The difference in productivity is huge. 4 people taking 6 minutes meant 24 minutes of total working time. That is now 1 robot taking one-and-a-half minutes. So the robot is 24/1.5 = 16 times more efficient.
With such a huge improvement in productivity the cost of producing a car falls, giving the business a competitive advantage and enabling it to make higher net profits.

Legislation and Business

What? (Grade 5 basics)

Legislation means laws passed by parliament. Laws affecting business include those concerning consumer rights, employment and health and safety. Businesses worry that legislation adds too much to their operating costs.

Why? (Grade 6)

For businesses operating within the European Union there is no problem, because all operate within the same laws. But UK businesses might be at a cost disadvantage compared with countries with weaker laws, such as America and less developed countries. British workers legally get 28 days' paid leave a year; in America the figure is zero. Does anyone in the UK really want to cut down on employees' holidays?

How? (Grade 7)

New laws affecting businesses set standards such as a minimum level of pay or a minimum standard for health and safety. In the UK 137 people died at work in 2016/17; in the equivalent figure for the USA was 5,190. Americans are eight times as likely to die at work than Brits.

So? (Grade 8)

Some politicians suggest that British business would be much better off without the 'burden of legislation'. In fact most businesses accept that current consumer, employment and health and safety laws are a strong basis for operating today. Many businesses want to beat the minimum standards set by law – such as offering all staff a salary that's above the national living wage.

Grade 9

In countries with few laws governing business, consumers and workers can suffer. In China in 2008 6 babies died and 54,000 ended up in hospital after suffering from contaminated baby milk. In the same year 100,000 workers were killed in workplace accidents. Since then China has passed tough employment and consumer laws. Of course, too may rules and regulations would stifle business enterprise, but there is little sign of that in the UK. The UK is regularly ranked in the top 10 countries in the world for ease of starting a business.

Do remember that legislation brings benefits as well as costs. Many companies see the benefit from having a 'level playing field'

Don't forget that UK business can – and do- have a big influence on UK legislation. Laws aren't simply imposed on them by nasty governments.

Exam tip: examiners like you to understand both sides to legislation. Yes it's good for customers and employees, but sometimes it may be extra work (and cost) for businesses.

Legislation: 5-step logic chain (to get to the top level of response)

Chain 1. If legislation such as the minimum wage was set at too high a level (1) … it might place such high costs on UK businesses (2) … that it became difficult to make a profit when competing with goods from other, low-wage countries (3). That might force a UK business to close down in the UK (4) and perhaps open a factory overseas. (5)

Chain 2. Business leaders have always complained about new legislation (1) … if they had been listened to there would still be children working in coal mines and up chimneys (2). More recently, businesses said the new minimum wage law (2009) would create waves of unemployment (3) … but happily that proved incorrect (4). Today, no-one wants child labour – and few want to return to poverty wages. (5)

The Economy and Business

What? (Grade 5 basics)

The economy affects businesses in many ways, largely through changes in:

- the levels of consumer income known as the economic cycle
- government policy towards the economy, e.g. a cut in taxes
- exchange rates, e.g. the £ rising in value against the U.S. dollar

Why? (Grade 6)

Changes in the economy can have serious effects on businesses when they are unexpected. A business spending big on a new, bigger factory may suddenly be hit by a 'recession'. Falls in consumer incomes throughout the economy lead to falling sales. So the company spending on growth is hit by falling revenues. Lower revenues and rising costs can squeeze profits dramatically.

How? (Grade 7)

The UK economy is affected sharply by what's happening in linked economies in Europe and America. If they are weak we sell fewer exports to them, so our businesses suffer. And if our government wants to follow 'austerity' policies such as cutting its spending on disability benefits – that cuts total consumer spending and therefore cuts business revenue.

So? (Grade 8)

Business bosses want to be in control. They like to establish their own objectives then plans to meet or beat them. Unexpected economic changes can get in the way. A rise in the value of the £ can ruin an exporter's target of boosting sales by 10%. Or a rise in inflation can eat away at consumers' spending power, cutting sales revenues for businesses throughout the country.

Grade 9

Businesses always try to influence the things they can't control. They try to persuade politicians of the economic policies that are 'right' for business and the economy: perhaps keeping interest rates low in order to keep consumer spending high. And they may push for cuts in unemployment pay, to force those without jobs to hunt for work. Sometimes the policies being pushed for are good for businesses and their shareholders, but less good for employees and less good for the long-term health of the UK economy.

Do be clear that economic change can overwhelm businesses. A sudden recession or a sharp fall in the £ can catch businesses out. Businesses want stability, not drama

Don't forget people. The exam questions are about businesses, but the answers are richer if you think about the impact upon people. So beware of seeming keen to see real people sacked.

Exam tip: examiners love you to know that businesses are affected differently by economic factors. Sales of toilet paper or ketchup are little affected by economic ups and downs. But sales of sports cars and other luxuries can be affected hugely

---

Economy and Business: 5-step logic chain (getting to the top response level)

Chain 1. When a recession hits or when interest rates rise sharply (1) ... consumer spending falls in response to worsening consumer and business confidence (2) causing consumers to be more cautious about spending (they'd rather save 'for a rainy day') (3) and businesses to cut back spending on new investments (4) creating a risk of job losses... and a further downturn in consumer spending (5).

Chain 2. If economic growth in Europe and America boosts our exports (1) ... and therefore UK business revenues (2) ... consumer and business confidence rises, providing more jobs and cutting unemployment. (3) If companies respond by increasing their spending on investment (4) the whole economy benefits, including more tax revenue flowing into the government's bank account. (5)

External Influences on Business

What? (Grade 5 basics)

An external influence is a factor outside the control of the business. Factors include changes in technology, legislation and the economic climate. All three have been dealt with in previous chapters; here we focus on possible responses by the business to these changes.

Why? (Grade 6)

This GCSE wants you to understand how changes in external factors influence the decisions businesses make. Success in business is tough at the best of times, as shown by the number of new businesses that fail – and the number of newly-launched products that flop. Changes in technology, legislation and the economy add extra layers of difficulty to business management.

How? (Grade 7)

Big businesses deal with these three factors by doing all they can to influence or control their impact. One example would be buying up the competitor that has developed the threatening new technology, as Google did with YouTube. Another example is the way big businesses provide funds to support the political parties that have economic or legislative policies that are believed to be helpful to companies.

So? (Grade 8)

Some responses will be pre-emptive, such as putting pressure on the government to drop a planned piece of environmental legislation. Others will be reactive, such as deciding what the company should do in response to a sharp rise in UK interest rates.

Grade 9

In exams it is crucial to understand the timescale suggested by the question. An exam text might cover the arrival of fully-tested, reasonably-priced self-drive cars within the next 3 years – then ask how a company such as Jaguar Land Rover might respond. It could wait until the actual products are launched and respond then (reactively), or it could start immediately – to prepare itself fully for the technological change. Surely the pre-emptive approach is more likely to succeed.

> **Do** think about the strength of the effects of the external factor. Economic change will hardly affect sales of socks, but may damage sales of luxuries such as sports cars

> **Don't** forget that these external factors add more difficulty to the already-tricky job of managing a business effectively. They make a tough job tougher.

> **Exam tip:**
> beware of overstating your case. Changes in business laws may disappoint some managers, but rarely if ever force a company into insolvency or 'going under'

External influences: 5-step logic chain (to get to the top response level)

Chain 1. If experts agree that the UK economy is set for strong growth (1) an online retailer might want to pre-empt this (2) ... by investing in more warehousing in more regions of the country (3) ... to cope with higher demand in future (4). It takes time to build new warehousing, so if it doesn't act now it may be too late. (5).

Chain 2. A new law might be passed that an entrepreneur hadn't noticed and therefore hadn't prepared for (1) ... which might lead to a prosecution, a guilty verdict and a fine (2). This might be embarrassing, though it's likely that few customers will notice (3) making the effect less serious than it might be (4). Fortunately in the UK most businesses want to meet all legal requirements. (5).

Answering exam questions

To give an idea of how to use the material on external influences, two questions re set out below, with the answers on the right. These are to help show how the subject matter can be used in the exam room.

Q1. Discuss how external influences might weaken the profits made by a family-owned seaside hotel. (6 marks)

Q2. Evaluate how an online retail business might respond to a sharp reduction in the amount of employment legislation affecting UK companies. (12 marks)

On the right are strong answers to these two questions. They focus on how external influences can be used in the answers – and the answer to Q2 can be regarded as a strong answer to a 12 mark question.

For more on exam technique see Section 3.

Grade 9 Answers (see questions on the left)

1. *Changes in consumer spending could be an important factor. If low-income families are made worse off by cuts to working tax credits, they may have to reduce or cancel their holidays. As low-income families are unlikely to afford foreign holidays, it will probably be seaside hotels that face a fall in bookings. And with a business such as a hotel, most of the costs are fixed, so a fall in revenues will mean a nasty drop in profits (as costs won't fall by much).*

A separate factor might be a failure on the hotel's part to cope with new technology. If the owners had ignored social media and online booking, the hotel might lose market share in the local town. Customers will book in the easiest and most convenient way possible.

2. The online retail business is likely to be pleased to have fewer laws to meet. It may no longer have to pay legally-set minimum wages, giving it scope to reduce costs. This would mostly affect low-skilled workers – perhaps those in the distribution warehouses that store, pick and pack customer orders. The online business may soon regret this cost-cutting however, as once-loyal staff may leave for other, better-paid jobs and young people may refuse to work for what they regard as 'poverty' wages.

Fewer employment laws might also end the legal requirement to provide paid maternity and paternity leave. This also may seem great to the business in the short-term, but prove a problem for the business over coming years, as young mums leave and don't return after having their babies. There may be fewer business benefits from ending employment legislation than some politicians wish to suggest.

Extra exam tip: the key issue about external factors is that they're outside the entrepreneur's control. That's ironic because that's why people start up on their own – to get more control of their working life ('Be my own boss'). Businesspeople hate to have uncertainty in this way – which explains much of the hot air surrounding Brexit. If businesses aren't sure what difference it's going to make, they worry – and in many cases try to affect the outcome by paying for involvement in politics.

Methods of growth

What? (Grade 5 basics)

A business can achieve growth from within (organic growth) or by external means such as buying up a rival company. Internal growth can come from developing new products or finding new customers in new markets. In both cases the planning and the effort comes from within the business, e.g. clever marketing staff finding a new type of customer.

Why? (Grade 6)

Internal growth is beneficial because your own staff are the ones developing the new opportunities. This is better than writing out a cheque to buy up a rival, because staff build careers based on their own success. Google has bought some other businesses, but most of its growth has come organically – which is why staff are so proud to work there.

How? (Grade 7)

To grow organically you need to understand your customers well enough to see what extra services they may require – and how their tastes may develop in future (think iPhone after iPhone). This may require big spending on consumer market research plus Research & Development to try to find innovative new products. A business that grows inorganically may be trying to cover up its own failings by buying up better rival businesses.

So? (Grade 8)

News programmes love a take-over because it means something exciting happening in the business world. But staff don't find it exciting to have their jobs threatened – and customers may hate to lose 'their' Cadbury or McVities to a foreign owner. So organic growth is much more likely to benefit the stakeholders in a business – and is also more likely to help the country's economic growth rate. Inorganic growth is over-rated.

Grade 9

The best thing about organic growth is that it tends to be slow and steady. It's like a twiggy young tree growing over the years into something substantial, with a strong trunk and a big canopy of green leaves and shoots. Buying up another business means a sudden leap forward in the company's size and scale – and many managers find that this is very hard to handle. A five-year-old may yearn to become an adult overnight – but it's hard to see it working out well.

> **Do** think about new markets as well as new products. It's still called organic growth even if it's a UK company opening its first outlets in China or Vietnam

> **Don't** make growth sound too easy. *Cash flow comes under serious pressure when businesses grow rapidly – such as when two companies merge*

> **Exam tip:** lots of exam questions cover private and public limited companies. Revise them with care. Remember that plcs can sell their shares on the stock market – to raise lots of extra capital

---

Methods of growth: 5-step logic chain (to get to the top level of response)

Chain 1. Growing successfully by takeover requires a huge amount of management skill (1) … perhaps more skill than most managers actually have (2). Growing organically is better because it's a bit slower and therefore more controllable (3) … and because it's built on the career success of your own staff (4) … just like a football team built on local talent, not bought-in from the outside. (5)

Chain 2. To grow organically, a business needs new ideas for products/services backed by new technology (1) … therefore making it hard for competitors to keep up (2) … allowing your organic growth to come from your increasing market share (3). Growing by looking overseas is risky (4) … for every success (Costa; Burberry) there are overseas flops (M&S; Tesco). (5)

Finance for growth

What? (Grade 5 basics)

Growth can be financed from within the resources of the business, e.g. from profit, or from outside. Internal sources of finance include retained profit and selling assets. External sources include loan capital and share capital. The most important is to convert from a small Ltd business into a big plc by 'floating' the shares on the stock market. This can raise £100s of millions overnight, such as Hotel Chocolat in 2016 or Snap (Snapchat) in 2017.

Why? (Grade 6)

Growth sounds such a good thing that it's hard to realise that it usually requires the investment of lots of cash. If retail orders this year are double last year's, a manufacturer has to spend on factory expansion, more machinery, materials and staffing. The cash inflows come later. So finance for growth must be planned early, to get agreements in place with bankers or investors.

How? (Grade 7)

The first choice is between internal and external sources. Internal sources may provide enough capital, if the business is highly profitable, customers pay on time and there are some unwanted but valuable assets that can be sold. But that would be quite rare. Usually external sources are also needed – either loan capital or share capital. Selling shares is a safe source of capital, but does risk losing control of the business. Loan capital means monthly interest payments plus repaying that capital – both drains on cash flow.

So? (Grade 8)

Decades ago, members of the Sainsbury and the Ford families made their kids and grandkids hugely rich by floating these businesses on the stock market, providing the finance for vast growth – to the financial benefit of everyone. It's understandable to want to hold on to 51% of the business you started up, but the business itself can benefit hugely from growth without debt.

Grade 9

The questions of internal v external capital, plus share capital versus loan capital (debt) are very important. More important than either, though, is to plan early to know how much cash you'll need to get the business to the next level. And when you go early to the markets – to a crowdfunding site, perhaps – it's much easier for people to trust that you know what you're doing – and therefore invest in you.

> **Do** think about the possibilities for raising finance by a flotation (selling share capital) rather than borrowing money from the bank. Bank borrowing is the riskiest form of finance.

> **Don't** forget that loan capital has an added level of uncertainty, because no-one knows what interest rates will be in a year or two's time

> **Exam tip**: when discussing sources of finance, the keys words are 'risk' and 'control'. Internal sources and also loan capital ensure you don't give away control – but perhaps at too high a level of risk

---

Finance for growth: 5-step logic chain (to get to the top level of response)

Chain 1. In business you pay today for cash inflows that come tomorrow (1) ... so growth needs to be financed with care – and cash (2). Most bosses start by looking at internal sources such as profits the business is making (3) ... but usually there's a need to look to external sources also (4) ... such as a careful balance between share and loan capital – to balance keeping control with the risk of debt. (5)

Chain 2. Growth is tricky to finance, but far worse is rapid growth (1) ... such as online fashion retailer Boo.hoo's 2017 growth rate of over 100% (2) The more rapid the growth the less likely that internal sources will provide much cash (3) ... because the speed of change is already such a financial drain (4). So rapid growth makes a flotation especially attractive – bringing in extra share capital (5)

Ownership for Growth

What? (Grade 5 basics)

There are three options within ownership for growth. One is to convert from an Ltd small business into a big Plc. That makes it possible to raise money via the stock market. Then there are two ways of growing by changing the ownership structure. One is to combine permanently with a business of similar size as a merger. The other is for a big business to take over a smaller one – perhaps adding 25% to the size of the business - instantly.

Why? (Grade 6)

Business bosses are often impatient. They want to achieve something big – perhaps becoming the No 1 in their market – and want to achieve it NOW! So instead of steadily working away at building market share, they make a take-over bid for a rival. If they succeed they may become Number 1 overnight. So external growth by takeover or merger can be very attractive.

Similarly, 'going public' can bring in £millions overnight. A private limited company converts into a plc and can then float its shares onto the stock exchange.

How? (Grade 7)

To take over another company you make a bid by offering a higher price per share than their current stock market value. So if the market price of your rivals' shares is £7, you might bid £9. If most of the rival's shareholders sell to you, you can achieve full control. To merge, you just need the agreement of the main directors and shareholders.

So? (Grade 8)

Takeovers can work out brilliantly for the companies, such as Google buying Youtube or Mars buying Wrigley's. In both cases they extended the company's reach into their market – and boosted profits. But Google itself has had several disasters, including buying Motorola for $12billion – then selling it for $3billion just two years' later. Even for a giant such as Google, a $9 billion loss hurts.

So takeovers should be undertaken with huge care. The same goes for mergers, which can also turn out badly.

Grade 9

No-one can be sure whether a takeover or merger will work out well or badly. But one thing is certain. If the takeover is financed by debt, the risks of failure become hugely greater. In January 2018 the huge Carillion construction group collapsed. It was weighed down by debts after going on a takeover spending spree.

> **Do** show the examiner you understand the risks involved in buying a business you don't know and understand. The 2010 take-over of Blackburn Rovers FC by an egg producer from India proved a disaster.

> **Don't** forget the possible impact of a takeover on the customers. They rarely gain.

> **Exam tip**: the exam board loves balanced answers and here's a great topic. Takeovers have positives but also many possible negatives. Good to remember for the conclusion that research shows that about two thirds of mergers & takeovers prove a disappointment

---

Ownership for Growth: 5-step logic chain (getting to the top response level)

Chain 1. A merger may seem a clever way out of a problem, e.g. when there are two struggling companies (1) ... but putting two messes together tends to make a bigger mess (2) ... because a bigger business is harder to manage (3). The biggest problems tend to be to do with staff morale and focus (4) ... so a positive sign is when the boss-to-be has a strong record at managing people. (5)

Chain 2. When a small business buys another the problems are especially bad (1) … because small firms are dominated by one individual – who usually feels like <u>the</u> expert (2) … so every idea from the outside is inevitably 'bad'(3) … leading to arguments and disputes (4)… which can rub off onto staff or customers – making the new combined business less pleasant to do business with. (5)

Answering exams

Edexcel produces sample exam papers to help teachers. In these there are two questions directly about takeovers. But in Edexcel's marking guidance there are plenty of mentions of takeovers. It is a topic that helps in answering many different questions about business strategy.

Here are 3 questions where changes in ownership are a significant part of the answer:

P2 Q7a) Define the term 'takeover'. (1 mark)

P2 Q7e) Evaluate whether Sainsbury's is likely to benefit from its takeover of Home Retail Group. You should use the information provided as well as your knowledge of business. (12 marks)

Q3. Discuss whether a fast-growing, family-owned online retailer should become a plc to help finance growth. (6)

On the right are strong answers to these three questions. They are models for writing about takeovers rather than models for how to score 6 or 12 marks.

For more on exam technique see Section 3.

Grade 9 Answers (see questions on the left)

7a) A takeover occurs when one company buys a majority of the shares in another company, thereby taking full control.

7e) *Sainsbury's took over Home Retail Group ('Argos') in order to strengthen its market position and profit. Figure 4 shows that Argos has almost as many stores as Sainsburys, but they make about a tenth of the profit. So putting some Argos stores into Sainsburys – to cut down on the number on the high street – seems a good one. It should cut out a lot of the fixed costs the business used to face.*

However, if Sainsbury was struggling with Lidl/Aldi while Argos was battling Amazon, perhaps the two businesses are too weak to get together. Perhaps they would each have been better off fighting their individual battles rather than trying to fight side-by-side. Two weak businesses rarely combine into one strong one.

On balance Sainsbury seems unlikely to benefit from this takeover. Research shows that most takeovers prove disappointing. It is hard to see why this should be any different.

Q3. Becoming a plc means that shares can be advertised to outsiders, perhaps by floating the company onto the stock market. This can bring lots of extra share capital – all at once. If growth is rapid, there's probably a need for a lot of extra finance – so this method would work.

However, selling shares to outsiders may mean losing the family's control of 50+% of the share capital. Down the line, others may be able to build a majority shareholding and get rid of the founder and other family directors.

Changes in Aims and Objectives

What? (Grade 5 basics)

The aims and objectives of a business are likely to change as a business develops. From a focus purely on survival the management may start to plan for growth. The aims and objectives may change in response to developments internally, such as the performance of the business and other internal reasons. Or there may be external factors such as changes in market conditions, technology or legislation.

Why? (Grade 6)

A business may start for personal reasons, such as to be your own boss. But once the business is up and running, the owner may want more – perhaps to develop a shop into a business empire, as happened with a coffee shop on Waterloo station called Costa. So objectives and ambitions change over time. They may also change because of circumstances, such as a sudden, exciting opportunity because of new legislation.

How? (Grade 7)

To set about changing your aims and objectives it's vital to talk long and hard with your key managers and staff. If they dislike your plans, they may need a rethink. If you're still sure, focus on how to achieve the objectives – and make sure every staff member knows their role.

So? (Grade 8)

The world is always changing, so it's important to rethink your objectives when market conditions or technology moves on. If an American tax cut opens up opportunities for UK exports, a new sales target may be called for. That should help motivate staff to take advantage of this situation, providing a big opportunity to boost revenue and profits.

Grade 9

However, there can be risks when aims and objectives change. Toyota spent 50 years building a reputation for the world's most reliable cars. Then the aim changed: to become the world's Number 1 carmaker. Quality took a backseat as the business launched new car models to make more sales. Suddenly, in 2010, a story broke about safety problems in Toyotas sold in America and China. The problems cost $billions to solve before the grandson of the original 'Mr Toyota' took back control and re-set quality and reliability as the key aims.

> **Do** think about factors relating to change, such as deciding whether to enter new markets, or exit existing ones. Rolls Royce once made marine (ship) engines, but decided to exit the market in 2018

> **Don't** ignore the effects of decisions such as exiting a market: this might mean reducing the workforce – with important effects on the people and families involved.

> **Exam tip:** remember that aims state where you want to go and objectives give clear signs of what you want to achieve and by when, e.g. increase market share to 22% by 2022.

Changes in Aims: 5-step logic chain (to get to the top level of response)

Chain 1. Sensible entrepreneurs start up with the aim of survival – to get through the super-tough first year (1) … but then may change to an aim such as to boost profit to over £50,000 a year (2). But even if the business has been going well, a sudden decline in market conditions might force a re-set back to survival (3) … perhaps by focusing on cash flow factors such as getting customers to pay promptly (4) to get through the tough period and then, later, re-focus on new, more positive, aims. (5)

Chain 2. If aims are switched from sales growth to profit growth (1) … it may be sensible to cut back on the product range. (2) If too many product lines are made it may be hard to keep control of costs and stock (3) … so cutting out the smaller-selling, less profitable lines can cut total costs (4) … making it easier to turn sales revenue into net profit. (5)

Business and Globalisation

What? (Grade 5 basics)

Globalisation is the increase in world trade that has brought the world's economies closer together. American imports such as Starbucks and iPhones are to be found in almost every country. And the UK has global exports such as whisky, Burberry coats and Ted Baker clothes. Some businesses such as HSBC bank may change the location of their Headquarters; HSBC moved from Hong Kong to London to help it become a global bank.

Why? (Grade 6)

The urge to operate globally comes from the huge opportunities in booming economies such as China. Between 2007 and 2017 car sales in the UK rose by 4%; in China they rose by 306%. Companies such as Jaguar Land Rover have to get into the Chinese market to have any long-term prospects. As well as China, India, Vietnam, Thailand and Indonesia are also growing rapidly.

How? (Grade 7)

Multinational companies such as Shell become global by opening oil refineries and petrol stations in many countries across the globe. Others achieve the same goal by keeping their roots firmly in the UK, but growing globally by exporting widely from the UK. ASOS – the online fashion retailer – has grown remarkably by showing a good understanding of young people worldwide.

So? (Grade 8)

During the period of rapid growth in world trade (1980-2008), extreme poverty in the world fell by 750 million, so globalisation seems to have been good for the world's poorest. So American President Trump's attack on trade in 2018 seemed odd. He imposed big tariffs (taxes on imports) on fridges and solar panels – hitting goods from China and South Korea especially. Although he justified his actions by saying "America First", the impact would have been to hit jobs and incomes in Asia (and to increase the price of fridges for American households).

Grade 9

Globalisation brings benefits to rich and poor countries alike. But there are also downsides. Some people hate to see a Starbucks and a McDonalds in every town in the world, as they'd like to see local, independent businesses thrive. And many worry that some multinationals are so rich and powerful that it's hard for governments to control them – and very hard to get them to pay their taxes. Overall, though, workers and consumers in poor countries welcome the arrival of a multinational that plans to open a factory or open shops nearby.

> **Do** think about the value to workers in poor countries of the chance of a job with a big multinational company – good training, good salary and better career prospects

> **Don't** doubt that some multinationals damage globalisation by their lazy approach to poorer countries' environment. Both Shell and BP have a poor record – especially in Nigeria and the US

> **Exam tip:** ASOS and Ted Baker have shown the power of UK fashion business in internet/e-commerce sales worldwide. Even smallish UK business may have the chance to compete internationally by clever use of e-commerce

---

Business and globalisation: 5-step logic chain (to get to top level of response)

Chain 1. Every UK business should look for global market opportunities (1) ... because countries such as China and India are growing faster than ours (2). A fully globalised business might try to produce new products designed for new markets, such as China (3) ... or open a factory in China, as Jaguar Land Rover has done (4). The key is to design products that are wanted (nearly) everywhere (5)

Chain 2. A UK company may decide to build sales in Asia or Africa by designing products for these markets (1) ... making it hard for competitors to keep up (2) ... unless they invest heavily in new products (3). In the past Marks & Spencer has struggled to sell profitably overseas. (4) ... perhaps because they wanted to sell UK items abroad instead of designing ones especially for local markets (5)

Ethics , the Environment and Business

What? (Grade 5 basics)

Ethical considerations affect a wide range of business decisions. The boss may know that the mainly-female accounts department is underpaid compared with mainly-male dispatch workers – but do nothing – hoping no-one notices. The boss may also know that the sales team's triumph in South America probably involved bribery – but do nothing. Both examples raise big ethical questions.

The environment also relies on morally sound business decisions. In the past, many businesses have thoughtlessly polluted rivers or damaged forests. Companies today are clearer that they are likely to get caught – and blamed.

Why? (Grade 6)

Ethics and the environment matter to shareholders when a company develops a poor reputation. After a huge oil spill in the Gulf of Mexico, BP sold off most of its U.S. operations – because American customers no longer wanted to deal with BP. And in a world of social media viral storms, no business should make itself vulnerable to sudden critical attacks.

How? (Grade 7)

From the first day, new staff should be told that the business cares about doing the right thing – and about its reputation. Staff should know that if they have a slight doubt about the ethics of a situation – they should ask their boss. And from the Directors there should be consistent evidence that ethics matter.

So? (Grade 8)

The most obvious ethical questions arise in ethics versus profit. If we cut out 25% of the sugar in our Coco Pops, will sales fall? Yes, but we think it's the right thing to do. Naturally, decisions such as that are very rare. Most companies hope to keep ethics 'quiet', while getting on with making money as usual.

Grade 9

The biggest test of a company's ethics is what it does when no-one's looking. Good companies get on with doing the right thing, even though no-one can see. Long ago, Marks & Spencer was like that: paying staff well and paying suppliers early. Companies that boast of their high standards deserve careful questioning.

> **Do** be willing to show the examiner that you care about ethics and/or the environment. It's fine to say that a company might make more profit doing one thing, but you think it's ethically proper to do something else.

> **Don't** hold back from criticising unethical companies, but remember that companies under financial pressure may cut corners to stay alive – not ideal, but perhaps forgivable

> **Exam tip**: when thinking of the environment, always think short-term (today's bad smells) versus long-term (global warming and sustainability). Poorly run businesses cover up the smells and don't deal with the long-term problems

---

Ethics & the Environment: 5-step logic chain (getting to the top response level)

Chain 1. A well-run business acts responsibly towards suppliers, customers, staff and pensioners (1) … which is easy to do if the company's profits are high enough (2). Therefore it's correct for the boss to focus on making the right decisions to generate high profits (3) … relying on other staff to make the right ethical decisions about the stakeholders (4) ... especially to look after the weakest(5).

Chain 2. Some small businesses only think about short-term profit (1) … such as the builder who illegally dumps waste by the roadside instead of paying for proper waste disposal (2). This is why laws exist to regulate business actions relating to the environment (3). The pressure to cut corners always exists in business (4)… making laws & regulations a helpful way to set out what's right and wrong. (5)

Answering exams

Exam questions on ethics or the environment are naturals for 6, 9 and 12-markers. Both topics are quite easy to develop into fuller answers.

Here are 3 questions featuring ethics and the environment:

Q1. Define the term 'ethics'. (1 mark)

Q2. Discuss the benefits to a business of taking care over the environment. (6)

Q3. Grayson's Ltd produces gluten-free doughnuts which are sold in all outlets of two large UK supermarket chains.

In order to improve its prospects for long-term growth, Graysons has two options:

Option 1. Higher ethical standards

Option 2. Higher profits.

Justify which one of these options Grayson's should choose. (9)

On the right are strong answers to these three questions. They are models for writing about ethics and the environment rather than models for how to score 6 or 9 marks.

For more on exam technique see Section 3.

Grade 9 Answers (Qs. on the left)

1. Moral standards in business.

2. A key environmental problem is finite resources. In other words the planet must eventually run out of materials such as copper. A business can help the environment by a 'lean' approach, minimising resource usage and wastage. This also means minimising business costs, therefore helping to build up profits.

A second benefit can come from repeat business due to customer loyalty. If customers see that a product if '100% recyclable' and boasts 'Two new trees planted for each one used' they may be willing to pay a little extra. Higher sales volume plus higher prices add up to a significant boost to revenue and profits.

Q3. To work to higher ethical standards could help the business be more attractive to stakeholders. Customers might be thrilled if the gluten-free dough was 100% organic, implying less stress on the environment. Indeed customers might be willing to pay a price premium – enough, perhaps, to cover the higher cost of ingredients. Staff would also be pleased partly because of the reassurance that their job has value, but also because of happier customers. The adoption of '100% organic' is not only ethically worthwhile, it adds sufficient value to pay for itself.

On the other hand focusing on ethics might be self-defeating. Gluten-free or not, a doughnut can never be the subject of much ethical respect. It's just yummy calories. If organic adds to the selling price demand may fall back to a small niche – making it hard to make a profit. There's nothing ethically impressive about business failure.

Product

What? (Grade 5 basics)

A successful product or service needs to be designed to meet customer needs and wants. This usually requires a careful balance between three things: function (how it works), aesthetics (how it appeals to the senses) and the cost of production. If the target market is young, cash-poor students, the design must be simple enough to allow low-cost production and therefore low prices. If the product is well enough designed it should have a long product life cycle – thanks to customers staying loyal for many, many years.

Why? (Grade 6)

Products must be well designed because they are at the heart of the marketing mix. Pricing, place and promotion cannot help if the product is dreadful. So companies can take years to develop the product with the right design mix. The design of the first Tesla electric car focused on aesthetics and function, with little regard for economic manufacture. Therefore it was expensive to make, and carried a high price tag, but quickly became the world's best-selling plug-in electric car. In many market sectors, customers are prepared to pay for quality.

How? (Grade 7)

The best designs start with a great understanding of how consumer behave and think – so market research is a good starting point. Then comes research & development, to turn customers' thoughts and needs into a design that stands out from the crowd. But design is more than the look and feel – it must also cover function – how well the product achieves its purpose. Does the robotic vacuum-cleaner really clean well? And is it quiet enough to avoid scaring pets?

So? (Grade 8)

If the design balance is right, customers will happily pay prices that yield high profits. And that allows the product to have a long life cycle, backed by consistent advertising spending and money spent in maintaining high distribution levels. Eventually sales may flatten out (reach maturity), making it time to bring in an extension strategy to extend the product's profitable life cycle.

Grade 9

You will know that the ideal marketing mix is based on linking the '4Ps' cleverly. And that the 4Ps together must match the customer need or market gap. But generally it is wrong to think of the 4Ps as being of equal value. The most important is Product. If the right product (or service) has been designed correctly to meet the precise needs of the market segment – it will take some stopping. The other 3Ps must be built around the Product. If a stylish Product is aimed at 20-30-year-olds with high spending power, the Price can be high, the Promotion focused on social media plus high-impact cinema advertising and the Place being trendy shops plus online.

Do think about the horizontal axis on a product life cycle diagram, i.e. Time. Cadbury's Dairy Milk was launched in 1905 – and is still in its maturity phase. Some products last centuries, others last only weeks, eg Loom Bands

Don't forget that an extension strategy is a medium-long term plan for extending the profitable life of a product.

Exam tip: make sure you can see how Market Research, Research and Development and the design mix link together. And never confuse M.R. with R&D.

Product: 5-step logic chain (necessary to get to the top response level)

Chain 1. A well-designed Product is at the heart of a successful marketing mix (1) … especially if the design mix helps in finding the right balance between aesthetics, function and costs. (2). Good design adds value to a product, partly through distinctiveness (3) … which, in turn, helps to keep customers loyal (4) … and forms the basis for building a powerful brand name. (5)

Chain 2. A short product life cycle may be measured only in months (1) … forcing the business to work constantly on new products to replace older ones entering their decline phase (2) … which adds to R&D costs and makes it hard to automate production processes (3). Longer life cycles make it easier to spread profits over the years (4) … putting less pressure on short-term profits (5).

Answering exams

It would be wise to expect regular exam questions on Product, the Design Mix and the Product Life Cycle. Here are two possible exam questions; possible answers are on the right.

Q1. Which **one** of the following is an element of the design mix?

A Cost

B Quality

C Promotion

D Price   (1 mark)

Q2. In order to improve its competitive advantage, Argos has two options:

Option 1: Lower prices

Option 2: Increase the speed of home delivery

(d) Justify which one of these options Argos should choose.

(9 marks)

On the right are strong answers to these two questions.

For more on exam technique see Section 3.

Grade 9 Answers (Qs. on the left)

1. Answer A: *Cost*

2. The case for Option 2 is strong if research has shown speed of delivery to be matter greatly to the customer. If so, it can be part of the design mix for the service, with the benefits of speedy delivery set carefully against the cost involved. An effective design mix gets the right balance between 3 factors, though in this case aesthetics (of delivery?) seem irrelevant. The balance has to be struck between speed and cost.

The case against Option 2, however, is that speed of delivery may bring only a very short-term competitive advantage. It's too easily copied by others. Argos faces direct competitors such as John Lewis and the might of Amazon – so speedy delivery is unlikely to bring an advantage for long.

On balance, the case remains strong for the faster delivery because although it may not be an advantage for long, without doing it we'll be leaving things open for rivals to do it first – leaving Argos behind.

Price

What? (Grade 5 basics)

Pricing strategies control the broad pricing decisions made by managers over the medium-long term. Arsenal season tickets, for example, have long been the most expensive in Europe.

When launching a new product, companies face a choice between three strategies:

- 'Skimming', which means pricing high to get high profit margins, even if sales volumes are fairly low
- 'Penetration', meaning to gain high volume sales by pricing low
- 'Competitive', meaning to price at the levels set by others already in the market

The choice of pricing strategy will have a huge effect on sales, market share and profits.

Why? (Grade 6)

The value of a clear pricing strategy is that customers can get used to it. Arsenal supporters may grumble, but learn to accept the price of their support. Fans of Primark will go out of their way to buy low-priced fashion. So the pricing strategy becomes part of the brand image.

How? (Grade 7)

If a new product is to be launched, managers must get a clear idea of its target market and the potential competition. If the target market is young, fashion and trend-conscious adults, a skimming strategy may work well. Even more so, if there's no direct competition. Careful market research is needed to get a clear understanding of the target customer – their habits, attitudes and spending power. Other influences on pricing strategies include technology and the product life cycle.

So? (Grade 8)

Even if a business has chosen a successful pricing strategy for the birth phase of a product's life cycle, it doesn't mean the strategy must always stay the same. A penetration strategy might have been right for the Nintendo Switch when launched in 2017. But its sales success may be so strong that a decision is taken later to push the price level up. So by the time it reaches its maturity phase, the pricing may have moved towards a skimming strategy.

Grade 9

A consistent medium-term strategy can establish a price as the 'right' one in the mind of customers. They can learn to believe that Chanel No 5 perfume is 'worth' £70 for 50ml, even though perfumes are quite cheap to produce. The worst approach to pricing is to be inconsistent, with high prices one week and deep price cuts the next. Customers learn to wait for the bargain prices – and lose their faith in the brand image.

Do remember that the word strategy means medium-long term (the word 'tactic' is used for short-term thinking such as a price promotion). So pricing strategies should run for years (or for ever in the case of Chanel No 5 perfume).

Don't assume that low prices are always a good thing. Companies need profits – and cutting prices can make the business unprofitable.

Exam tip: when reading about the business Edexcel has chosen, think about whether you would set high or low prices for the product or service. Write your thoughts alongside the text.

Price: 5-step logic chain (necessary to get to the top response level)

Chain 1. A brand new, highly innovative product/service should have a skimming strategy (1) … allowing prices high enough to give strong profit margins (2) … which can help finance further development work to create even better products in future (3). In effect this has been Apple's approach with its iPhones (4) … creating a virtuous circle of great products …. Strong prices … funding even better products … at even higher prices. (5)

Chain 2. A trained hairdresser may want open a store in their home town, even though there are already 8 established rivals (1) … forcing the new business to decide whether to price competitively or to undercut the others with penetration pricing (2). A decision to price similarly to competitors may make it a little harder to break in to the market (3) … but easier to make reasonable profits in the medium-long term (4) … as long as the hairdresser's talent keeps customers coming back (5).

Answering exam questions

Questions about pricing come up regularly on Business exams. In a single set of Edexcel's 'specimen' exam papers, the words price or pricing were mentioned 26 times in the mark scheme. This shows the importance of this topic. Here are two possible exam questions:

Q1. Explain one pricing strategy that might be successful for a new pizza delivery business.   (3 marks)

Q2. Fender is a producer of expensive guitars used by stars such as Bruno Mars.

Analyse the impact on Fender of charging high prices for its musical instruments. (6 marks)

On the right are strong answers to these two questions.

For more on exam technique see Section 3.

Grade 9 Answers (Qs on the left)

1. As there are lots of pizza delivery businesses in almost every town, penetration pricing would be best. It will enable the business to carve out a share of the market by undercutting the prices of rivals. Once established, it can push prices up a little.

2. Stars such as Bruno Mars probably want to use a guitar that is priced out of the reach of ordinary customers. It would reinforce the image of stardom to have an exclusive, special guitar. So pricing high should help in achieving consistent sales among a small niche market of professional musicians. This should provide enough revenue to cover costs and a large enough profit to finance the continuing growth of the business.

Like any other business, Fender would want to develop – perhaps into more technologically advanced guitars. Good profits based on high prices can enable it to do this.

Promotion

What? (Grade 5 basics)

Promotion means all the ways in which a business tries to persuade customers to buy: either now or in the future. The key to long-term success is branding, usually backed by image-building advertising and/or sponsorship. To boost today's sales businesses use special offers including product trials (handing out free samples). Special offers can be promoted cheaply by social media or e-newsletters – with every company hoping for such an exciting offer that it 'goes viral'. The key to success is selecting the right promotional strategy for the targeted segment.

> **Do** remember that promotion is expensive. A single 30 second TV commercial can cost £250,000 – and you need lots to make an impact

Why? (Grade 6)

The need to identify the appropriate promotion strategy is because there are huge costs involved. SpecSavers spends nearly £50 million a year on promotion in the UK alone. So advertising must be carefully targeted at the right audience. Every advertisement watched by someone with great eyesight is a waste of the company's money.

> **Don't** focus too much on special offers. Yes, they can boost sales, but just for a short time. Companies want sales to grow steadily over time

How? (Grade 7)

The first decision is whether to focus on long-term promotion of the brand, or boosting short-term sales. Then a decision is needed on whether to focus on traditional advertising such as TV, or digital advertising via Google or social media. But it all depends on how much the business can afford to spend. Small businesses with little to spend on promotion may simply put leaflets through doors locally.

So? (Grade 8)

As promotion is so expensive, targeted advertising online is very attractive to companies. Advertising for stairlifts only pops up in front of older internet surfers; advertising for Nike appears in front of sports-loving under-35s. The ability to learn about individuals' tastes – and to target them accordingly – makes digital advertising better value and less wasteful than TV commercials.

> **Exam tip:** when thinking about promotion, consider the link between the brand name and image and the way the product is advertised. With the best companies, they go together perfectly

Grade 9

Every, literally every, business will say that the best form of promotion is word-of-mouth (or the Twitter equivalent). In other words you want to give customers such a great experience that they come back – and recommend you to others. It's not only free advertising, it's also the most powerful type.

Promotion: 5-step logic chain (to get to the top level of response)

Chain 1. A new business may have very little money to promote their first product or shop (1) … making it vital to target the right people cost-effectively (2). That may mean low-cost leaflets through letter boxes (3) … or a big effort to create a social media presence (4) … but the business must make every effort to turn customers into fans – as nothing is as cost-effective as word-of-mouth recommendation (5)

Chain 2. To build up its brand name Just Eat spent heavily on posters and TV from early on (1) … to help customers understand that the Just-Eat website was the place to look when hungry (2). Now the business uses online media rather more (3) … to target fast-food-lovers and to inform existing customers of special offers (4). As a product life cycle develops the type of promotion can change. (5)

Place

What? (Grade 5 basics)

Place means the methods of distribution that get products from the factory to the consumer. This might be via retailers or e-tailers. For a market-leading brand such as Heinz Beans, getting and keeping distribution is not hard – every grocery shop wants Heinz on the shelf. But for lesser brands such as Branston Beans or for a brand new producer, Place can be a huge problem, i.e. persuading shops to find shelf-space for your product.

Why? (Grade 6)

Whereas online 'e-tailers' can have their warehouses where rents are low, shops need to be where people go – where rents are expensive. So shops have to keep stocked with high-selling products – and may be wary of taking a risk with a new, unknown brand. If it sells badly it's a waste of valuable shelf-space.

How? (Grade 7)

To persuade shops to stock your product you need to offer good credit terms ('please buy 20 packs today – we'll wait 2 months before sending the bill') and a big discount off the retail price. The shopkeeper needs to make a profit. Strong established brands are in a much stronger position, and will offer lower discounts and shorter credit periods.

So? (Grade 8)

For new businesses, Place is often the most difficult of the '4Ps'. Just at the time the business is shortest of cash, shopkeepers demand long credit terms – and big discounts off the price. And even when you've managed to sell to a retailer such as Sainsbury's, the shop managers demand that you meet ambitious sales targets – otherwise the product gets 'de-listed', i.e. withdrawn from the shelves and sent back to the factory.

Grade 9

There are lots of reasons why e-commerce online retailing can be more profitable than a high-street shop with a big rent bill and big local business taxes. But shops can still be important. Superdry wants to show you its full range of products in the setting it has chosen for itself. Then, perhaps, you'll decide to buy it online from the Superdry.com. So today's shops can be showrooms as well as taking in cash.

Do think about the difference between retailing and e-tailing. More than 25% of clothes are now bought online – and well over 50% of books.

Don't doubt the power of retailers such as Tesco. Recently they've been refusing to stock products even from major producers such as Pepsi. Keeping your place can be as hard as getting it.

Exam tip: examiners like you to be aware that place is nothing without profit. So it is not worth slashing your prices just to get distribution. Better to be in 50 shops profitably than 500 unprofitably.

Place: 5-step logic chain (to get to the top level of response)

Chain 1. A business with a good product that struggles to get distribution might build a website for e-commerce sales (1) ... thereby keeping the profit margin that used to be taken by the shops (2). The extra profit can be used to build up the website to make it better and better (as ASOS has done over the years) (3) ... and to promote the site using social media (4). Therefore make it the best Place for buying online (5).

Chain 2. For a new business offering an innovative new product (1) ... it should be possible to persuade trendy shops to try it out (2). The problem then is to persuade enough customers to buy that the shops keep the product in distribution (3). This is easier if the shops give the product a great display space, such as next to the checkout (4). They'll be willing to do that if they get a generous discount off the price, and therefore a big profit margin (5).

Marketing Mix and Making Decisions

What? (Grade 5 basics)

There are two key issues here: the importance of pulling the 4 elements of the mix together to make a coherent strategy; and using the mix to build competitive advantage. Business decisions might include finding the right marketing mix to challenge a successful rival; or changing the mix when the life cycle moves from growth to maturity.

Why? (Grade 6)

Ultimately, business is about making decisions. Not all will be right, but a manager who gets two thirds right can probably sleep securely. As all business decisions are about the future, the results are always uncertain. So an intelligently planned marketing mix may prove unsuccessful – there's no shame in that. Where there should be shame is when the mix is poorly coordinated, leaving customers and staff unsure of the product's image and credibility.

How? (Grade 7)

Start with careful market research; make a clear decision about the target market segment – then build a well-planned marketing mix focused on that target. This is how Nintendo's Switch became a success – by targeting customers other than the core market young, male fans of PS4 or Xbox One.

So? (Grade 8)

Business is not about quick wins, it's about building something. ASOS was floated on the stock market in 2001 for 20p. In February 2018 the shares were over £70. Someone who had invested £1,000 in 2001 would have had £350,000 by 2018. ASOS established a competitive advantage by being first into the online fashion clothing business – and sustained their advantage over newcomers. So marketing decisions that lead to a sustainable competitive advantage can be worth a fortune.

Grade 9

Gaining a competitive advantage over your rivals is difficult; sustaining it for years is even harder. Jealous rivals copy what's working for you – so the only way to stay ahead is to keep innovating. The ASOS website today is a brilliant development on the past, making full use of social media and the development of a Selfie culture. Getting ahead is clever; staying ahead is brilliant.

> **Do** show your understanding that marketing must be based on consumer wants and needs. A well-thought-out marketing mix points the product in the right direction, backed by the other 3 mix elements.

> **Don't** wreck an answer by pulling one element of the mix away from the rest. If the product and promotion are stylish and classy, don't suggest a bargain price!

> **Exam tip**: the examiner seems to love those two words: competitive advantage. See how both the logic chains given on the left build towards that precious phrase.

The Mix and Decisions: 5-step logic chain (getting to the top response level)

Chain 1. To stop sales sliding for Kellogg's Special K an extension strategy is needed (1) … by changing the image to focus on 'special', e.g. 'Special K – for when you've done something special' (2). This changes the promotional message (3) … and perhaps the pack design should have some gold as well as red (4). A well-integrated marketing mix could give Special K a new competitive advantage (5).

Chain 2. Faced with whether to launch a new product that has shone in research (1) … a key issue is if all 4 elements of the marketing mix point firmly towards the target customers (2). If one element looks weak the whole package may fail (3). If that one problem can be overcome, perhaps by going online (4) … it should be possible to build a long-term competitive advantage for the business (5).

Answering exams

Edexcel produces sample exam papers to help teachers. In these there is one question directly about the marketing mix and competitive advantage. But in Edexcel's marking guidance there are plenty of mentions of competitive advantage as a way of answering other questions.

Here are 3 questions where the mix and competitive advantage are being tested:

Q1. Explain how a small business could build a lasting competitive advantage.

Q2 (from P2, Q7d of Edexcel's Specimen Paper):

In order to improve its competitive advantage, Argos has two options:

Option 1: Lower prices

Option 2: Increase the speed of home delivery

(d) Justify which one of these options Argos should choose. (9 marks)

Q3. Discuss whether a business can succeed if its marketing mix is poorly integrated. (6)

On the right are strong answers to these three questions. They are models for writing about the topic rather than models for how to score 6 or 9 marks.

For more on exam technique see Section 3.

Grade 9 Answers (see questions on the left)

Q1. By finding an innovative way to open up a new, small market segment where it is the number 1 – and can make enough profit to keep making innovative changes to stay ahead of others.

Q7d) If Argos lowers its prices it will probably enjoy a period of rising sales and market share. Its rivals may be reluctant to copy these price cuts – and may wait to see what happens. If the Argos price cuts have little effect on their own sales, they'll keep their prices the same. Argos will be delighted. But if the Argos price cuts are having a serious effect on rivals' sales, they will surely have to respond. And if every company cuts its prices, consumers will be delighted but the companies will all suffer falling profits.

On the other hand, as long as sales volumes at Argos rise, the directors may be happy. With higher sales they'll be able to negotiate bigger discounts from their suppliers, bringing variable costs down. That may help ensure that even if prices are down, profits won't be.

Q3. If the mix is poorly integrated it will always be difficult for customers to understand the marketing and branding. Mercedes might have a wonderful Product at a high Price and distributed in the right (posh) Place, but if it ran a Buy One Get One Free promotion on the cars, the image would be wrecked.

However, if the business has no rivals, this may hardly matter, e.g. Tesla cars, before any other producer made an exciting, expensive electric car. So yes, a business can succeed for a while even if its marketing mix is poorly integrated, but when serious competition arrives it will have to rethink its marketing strategy and mix.

Business Operations

What? (Grade 5 basics)

The purpose of business operations is to produce goods and services. That means managing the whole process from buying materials through production to customer delivery. There are three different types of production process: job, batch and flow. Most large businesses try to use flow production as often as possible. Small businesses use job or batch production.

Why? (Grade 6)

Flow production is used when a single product can be produced continuously on a conveyor belt production line – preferably 24/7. A good example would be Heinz Beans. The highly automated UK production lines produce 1.5 million tins **a day**. Very little human labour is involved in the process, making the labour cost per tin extremely low, giving huge scope for high profits. Job production is used by small companies that tailor-make products to individual customer needs. In this case the labour cost will be high, so this can only work if the customer is willing to pay a high price – for a tailor-made wedding dress, for example.

How? (Grade 7)

To decide between job, batch and flow the business needs to consider the needs and wants of customers within the target market. Mercedes customers want to order a car tailored to their personal needs, so they provide thousands of options on each model. So flow production must be combined with job production (brilliantly, this is all done in an automated way on a largely robotic production line).

So? (Grade 8)

Business operations are rarely thought about by customers until something goes wrong. The wrong parcel turns up or the washing machine leaks. But many businesses build their reputation and brand name on their production excellence. And many more need to select the right production method (job, batch or flow) to help keep costs down and therefore keep prices competitive.

Grade 9

Large businesses like Apple want to make millions of identical phones cheaply. If they can sell them at high prices, that's a bonus. This provides an opportunity for small businesses to find niches the big companies aren't interested in. Then clever use of job or batch production makes it possible to provide exactly what the customer wants.

> **Do** think about the difference between products and services. Both need to be run efficiently, but services are more likely to be tailored to a customer's needs, while products are more likely to be mass-produced, by batch or flow.

> **Don't** ignore batch production, which means producing a set number of an identical item, e.g. 24 pairs of size 10 green dresses. Batch production provides limited scope for automation.

> **Exam tip:** remember, flow = low labour costs, but inflexible production; job = high labour costs but flexibility; and batch production is somewhere in the middle: quite flexible but quite costly.

Business Operations: 5-step logic chain (getting to the top response level)

Chain 1. Successful business operations need to combine good purchasing, the right production process and attention to quality (1) … all directed at what the customer wants or needs (2). When businesses get this right they are able to compete with the best, anywhere in the world (3) … and provide workers and managers with secure, perhaps well-paid jobs (4). So operations managers have a big and important responsibility (5).

Chain 2. Small businesses often start by batch-producing small quantities of a range of goods (1) … perhaps finding independent shops willing to be brave with a new product range (2). But if Tesco decides to stock the products it may be necessary to cut the number of lines (3) … and switch to flow production in order to produce high volumes at low costs (4). Then it should be possible to provide Tesco with the high profit margins they look for from any product they sell. (5).

Answering exams

Edexcel produces sample exam papers to help teachers. In these there is one question directly about job production. But in Edexcel's marking guidance there are plenty of mentions of efficient business operations as a way of answering other questions.

Here are 3 questions where business operations and types of production method are being tested:

Q1. Explain how a business could benefit from more effective business operations. (3)

Q2 (from P2, Q5d of Edexcel's Specimen Paper):

Fender uses job production to manufacture its hand-made musical instruments.

Analyse the impact on Fender of using job production to produce these musical instruments. (6 marks)

Q3. Discuss the benefits to a business of using batch production. (6)

On the right are strong answers to these three questions. They are models for writing about the topic rather than models for how to score 6 marks.

For more on exam technique see Section 3.

Grade 9 Answers (see questions on the left)

Q1. It would be able to produce the right goods at the right time and get them delivered to the customer on time – all at a low enough cost to ensure that the business makes good profits.

Q7d) If Bruno Mars wants a Fender guitar, it makes business sense to make a guitar that is so perfectly tailored that he wants to play it all the time. More play means more photos showing the brand name 'Fender' – and hopefully more sales. Job production can add value by tailoring to one individual, allowing a higher price to be charged. This, then, can benefit Fender further if they re-invest the extra profits into even better training to ensure even better guitars.

Q3. Batch production allows some benefits from automation while still keeping production quantities down to the level of demand. However cheap it would be to produce 2,000 XXL orange T-shirts, if the potential demand if for 40 – that's the number that should be produced. Low costs mean nothing if the products can't be sold.

But for some products it's important to restrict supply, producing only ten of one item and ten of another. Batch production has flexibility, whereas flow production is always the same.

Batch production allows businesses to match output to the wide range of different customer requirements, needs and wants.

Technology and Productivity

What? (Grade 5 basics)

Productivity is a measure of efficiency. Not 'how much have we produced?' but 'how efficiently have we produced it?' Flow production allows huge volumes to be produced with relatively few workers involved – that's high productivity. And the main reason that flow production works is because of company investment in high-technology machinery, perhaps including robots.

Why? (Grade 6)

Companies invest in modern, high-technology production because robotics can provide all the things a business wants: high productivity, high quality and flexibility at a reasonable cost. If productivity rises, more can be produced for the same costs, allowing the business to choose between more competitive prices or rising profits.

How? (Grade 7)

To boost productivity in a job production system, 3D printing can be used. A 3D printer can be programmed to make every product made-to-measure to fit a particular need. In the past, job production meant human labour; today 3D printing is the high-tech answer. In flow production, as mentioned above, robots may be important, but it is the conveyor belt system (invented over 120 years' ago) that is the key factor.

So? (Grade 8)

To build a successful business you need profit. This is the key source of capital to fund stable growth. So production efficiency isn't a luxury, it's a necessity. It is the way to boost efficiency, cut production costs and thereby allow the business to not only compete, but perhaps also start to beat the competition. If the company profit is invested wisely into updating machinery throughout the production process (plus extra training for staff) the profits should keep coming in future.

Grade 9

In the short term staff fear that greater investment in technology might mean fewer jobs. It would be silly to think that's never happened before. But despite waves of automation over recent decades there are more jobs today than ever before. So it's fair to expect that in the medium-long term there's probably no stopping the advance of technology – and no reason to fear that robots will be taking all the jobs in future.

> **Do** think about the benefits of technology. Twenty years' ago the paint on new cars was sprayed on by workers in constant danger of inhaling the spray. With robots it doesn't matter.

> **Don't** confuse 'productivity' with 'production'. Some people think that productivity is a posher was of saying production. It isn't; they're different. Production is output; productivity is efficiency.

> **Exam tip:** examiners are impressed by students who know that the higher the productivity, the lower will be the labour cost per item produced. So a _fall_ in productivity pushes _up_ labour costs per unit.

Technology & Productivity: 5-step logic chain (to get the top level of response)

Chain 1. One way to boost productivity is to invest more on training (1) … which will help boost staff morale and motivation as well as effectiveness (2). If staff then work harder and smarter (3) … they will get more work done per day (4) … which is the definition of productivity (5).

Chain 2. Spending more on modern technology such as robots (1) … generates more output per worker (2) ... and therefore boosts efficiency, as long as there is enough production to keep the robot working. (3). However with a small business a robot may only need to operate for a third of the day (4) … so the robot's purchase cost may not make financial sense (5).

Managing Stock

What? (Grade 5 basics)

Stock is made up of two main elements: ingredients and materials waiting to be turned into products; and 'finished goods' – ready to be delivered to customers. Modern businesses like to use just-in-time (JIT) methods of stock control. They operate with as little spare stock as possible. In the past, supermarkets had stock rooms, where spare products sat waiting for when needed. Today's supermarkets put new stock straight onto the shelves – and have no back-up in case there's a sudden rush to buy extra strawberries, or the cream to go with them.

Why? (Grade 6)

At the end of its 2017 financial year, Jaguar Land Rover had £3,500 million of 'stock'. Much of that was parts and components waiting to be fitted to cars – and much more was finished cars waiting to be delivered to customers. With so much money involved, managing stock has to be taken very seriously.

How? (Grade 7)

The basic model for controlling stock can be shown as a diagram: the bar gate stock graph (shown below). This shows the finished stocks of 'Superwarm' gloves at a warehouse. The managers always want a minimum of 100 pairs in stock, but have decided to cut their maximum stock level from 500 pairs to 300. This may be a stepping stone towards a plan to move to a JIT system.

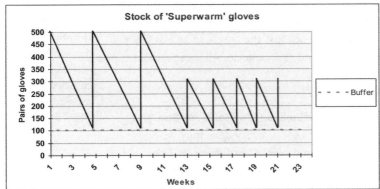

So? (Grade 8)

The more stock a business holds, the more of its own cash is tied up in that stock. As businesses can find plenty of other ways to use cash, companies try to keep stocks low. The higher the stock level, the less cash the business will have to run itself day-by-day. Therefore cutting stocks generates cash and improves cash flow.

Grade 9

ASOS and Zara both try to operate with very low stock levels. This is because clothing fashions are always changing. So they don't want to be left with big stocks of yesterday's fashions. Stocks not only tie up cash, they can also represent poor buying decisions – piling up on the clothing racks – and needing to be sold off cheaply in the next Sale.

Do remember that stock has two elements: 'goods in' such as raw materials and 'goods out', i.e. the finished product. With goods in, the easiest way to cut stocks is to order less from suppliers. With goods out, you need more orders from customers.

Don't assume that cutting stocks cuts costs and therefore boosts profit. Stocks affect cash, not profit. So if a business needs to boost its cash flow, cutting stocks is an excellent method.

Exam tip: the bar gate graph will come up regularly in exams. You might be asked to identify the reorder quantity (400 gloves in weeks 1 - 11; 200 after week 13) or the minimum stock level (100).

Managing stock: 5-step logic chain (to get to the top level of response)

A manufacturer planning to cut stock levels should move to JIT (1) ... though it will be difficult at the start (2) ... because buffer stocks fill in for any production shortfalls (3). Without a buffer, every delayed delivery halts production and delays deliveries to customers (4) .. which may lead to lost customers and falling market share (5).

The Role of Procurement

What? (Grade 5 basics)

Procurement means obtaining supplies. Businesses usually negotiate with a number of suppliers, then decide on the basis of quality and reliability, costs and credit terms. Some companies offer the business to just one supplier in order to get the best possible terms. A supplier with the chance of a huge contract may offer especially low prices.

Another factor is logistics: the organisation of transport and delivery of stock plus the final deliveries to customers. Efficient logistics help to keep costs down while ensuring the reputation of the business and a high level of customer satisfaction.

Why? (Grade 6)

In 2018 the huge aircraft-maker Airbus found problems with engines supplied by one of the top American engine-makers. Fortunately it had a deal with a second supplier. By switching to the second supplier, customer airlines could keep getting deliveries of their planes. Clever procurement saved Airbus from cancellations on its orders. With each A320 airplane priced at $101 million, this is no small matter.

How? (Grade 7)

Procurement starts by identifying the exact supply needs. In 2018 Airbus received an order for 36 A380 Superjumbo airplanes from Emirates Airlines. Delivery begins in 2020, so Airbus must place orders for 36 sets of aero-engines from key suppliers. Negotiations with suppliers may take a long time, because each engine costs around $50 million. And in this case, it's not just the purchase and delivery that matters, but also the after-sales service and maintenance. All these factors can be part of the procurement decision.

So? (Grade 8)

Successful businesses such as Toyota or Jaguar build up long-term relationships with key suppliers. Instead of fighting over the cost of every deal, they work together on improving quality plus the speed and reliability of delivery. The important thing is to build up trust, so that the producer has faith in the supplier. For example, if the supplier is struggling to keep up with orders, it should inform the customer in plenty of time about the threat to the availability of the supplies.

Grade 9

With the rise in online e-commerce, procurement and logistics are becoming a central part of management. Millions may be spent on advertising, but if the customer gets the wrong product delivered, she won't return. The 2018 KFC disaster (outlets closures/chicken delivery problems) will not be forgotten quickly.

Do remember that procurement can be done in one of two ways: switching suppliers regularly, to whichever is the cheaper; building a relationship over time to work with a supplier on new innovations and ever-better quality

Don't forget 'logistics' – the management of transport and delivery to keep costs down and customer satisfaction up.

Exam tip: don't muddle logistics and procurement; examiners love to see business terms used in exactly the right way.

Procurement and Logistics: 5-step logic chain (to get to the top response level)

Chain 1. For a business with weak profits, costs can be cut by more careful procurement (1). There are advantages in having the same supplier for 20 years, but it's important to check, every few years, to see what else is on offer (2). Britain leaving the E.U. gives an opportunity to look again at possible UK-based suppliers (3) … who may be able to supply more cheaply thanks to lower transport costs (4) … allowing better procurement to help cut costs and re-build profits. (5)

Chain 2. For a fast-expanding business logistics can be a problem (1) .. because it's hard to get enough trucks, lorries and drivers (2) … to keep inward supplies and customer deliveries arriving on time (3). So it's important to hire a really capable Logistics Manager – and give her or him the power to make decisions such as buying new trucks (4) … without checking every decision with senior managers (5)

Managing Quality

What? (Grade 5 basics)

Quality means different things to different people. For me, ice cream must be dairy; for you, it may have to be dairy-free. But we can both love ice cream. What links us, though, is that we want a good example of the ice cream we like. If the tub has been part-melted then refrozen in transit, we'll both find the texture disappointing, unpleasant even. So quality is to deliver the product the customer expects, i.e. to meet or beat expectations. To achieve this there are two main methods: quality control (Q.C.) and quality assurance (Q.A.).

Do think about the importance of quality in the service sector. Hot food is wrecked if it's delivered cold, and a holiday ruined if the water in the pool is cloudy.

Why? (Grade 6)

Why are there two methods for achieving quality? Largely because quality control is used by organisations that doubt their staff and therefore want to check everything before it's sent out. Quality assurance works by trusting staff to check their own work at every stage in the process, with the hope that no mistakes will get through to the end of the production line.

Don't muddle Q.A. and Q.C. Most modern businesses try to build quality into every stage in the production process: so that's Q.A.

How? (Grade 7)

To organise a quality control system you need to appoint quality inspectors who understand the product well enough to spot imperfections. They operate at the end of the production line to stop poor quality work slipping through to customers. But whereas you can look and see whether a car door fits well, it's harder to know if a car will stay reliable over the years. Quality assurance is better for dealing with what the inspectors cannot see. A well run Q.A. programme has all staff trying their best to provide high quality output.

So? (Grade 8)

Today, quality is taken for granted in most business settings. You expect your fries to be hot and crisp and your Coke to be cold. Businesses that fail to provide quality are likely to struggle. So quality is important not because it takes you to the front of the pack, but because it stops you falling behind. What distinguishes Nike from New Balance is not quality – it's design and image.

Exam tip: the examiner has highlighted the link between high quality and cost control – and therefore competitive advantage. That's a wonderful link for exam answers.

Grade 9

If quality management is effective, no time will be wasted re-working poorly-fitting parts, and no money will be wasted on reject products that must be scrapped. This allows businesses to control costs and gain a competitive advantage.

Managing quality: 5-step logic chain (to get to the top level of response)

Chain 1. If sales are slipping it's sensible to check how customers rate the product's quality (1) … and the service level that's supports the product (2). A switch from Q.C. to Q.A. may be called for, because quality assurance helps in building quality into every stage in production (3) … making it easier to cut wastage costs (4) … which can build a competitive advantage and help re-build sales (5).

Chain 2. If all the products in your market are produced to high quality standards you may need to boost your image by better design (1) … because there's more to quality than reliability (2). iPhone users love the quality feel that's been designed in (3) … which adds value (4) … enabling significantly higher prices to be charged (5)

The Sales Process

What? (Grade 5 basics)

Many products sell themselves, such as a Cornetto on a hot day. But others need selling, either because of complexity or because the key consumer benefits are not obvious. For a product as complex as a modern smartphone, older customers especially need a quick lesson on how the phone works. And the car buyer may not realise there's a warranty guaranteeing free servicing for 3 years.

Why? (Grade 6)

The importance to businesses of providing good customer service comes, in the short-term, from the ability to turn a customer inquiry into a customer order; after all, that's the only thing that generates revenue. In the long term, good service is about getting first-time customers to become regular – and getting those same people to mention you to others ('word-of-mouth' or 'viral' benefits). A website says research exists showing that 68% of lost customers 'felt poorly treated'. So the sales process must focus on great customer service.

How? (Grade 7)

Sales staff need terrific product knowledge, so they can answer every question, the personality to engage with customers, plus the speed and efficiency to make sure that the customer gets exactly what they want, without delay. Then, after the sale has gone through, the salesperson needs to pass on important customer feedback (the chicken was a bit too salty; the range of colours on offer was disappointing) as well as handle after ('post')-sales service.

So? (Grade 8)

If customer service is vital, then training and motivating sales staff is equally so. Time-after-time banks have been guilty of giving sales staff commission payments that encourage them to oversell. In other words bank staff sell expensive financial products to people who don't really need them. This is immoral, but is also bad business. Staff should be trained to say no to a customer who wants a product they don't need; and in that way create trust not anger. But if financial incentives are often a foolish way to over-incentivise staff, the motivation to provide great service is a wonderful thing.

Grade 9

Customers love to be understood – to be pampered when they want it, but also to be dealt with quickly and efficiently when that's what's needed. The best sales person understands customer body language to see which approach is required. That hinges partly on the salesperson's intelligence, but can also be a lot to do with good training.

Do think hard about the business situation. Sales and service are very different in a car showroom, a Lidl and for an online shop. Your exam answers must be adapted to the situation you face – just as in the real business world.

Don't play down 'customer engagement'. This is the potential magic that takes good service (a smile, perhaps a handshake) into something special: real warmth, remembering your name, or giving a free sample - fresh from the oven.

Exam tip: examiners want you to realise there has to be a balance. If great service adds too much to costs, then either prices must be increased or profits may be hit. But genuine smiles are free.

The Sales Process: 5-step logic chain (getting to the top response level)

Chain 1. For a new business like a café every customer is precious (1). The target is to turn as many as possible into regulars (2) ... by a sales process that goes beyond efficient towards something special (3). Ideally, customers will then go out of their way to come to you (4) ... providing a steady, stable income to help move the business beyond its break-even point (5).

Chain 2. With an online business the sales process is different (1) … with a greater emphasis on simplicity and efficiency (2). Placing an order in two clicks would mean wonderful speed and efficiency of service (3) … and the post-sales service must also be great – making it easy to send back unwanted items (4). Customer engagement is not important; speed, simplicity and efficiency take over (5).

Answering exams

Edexcel produces sample exam papers to help teachers. In these there is one question directly about customer service. But in Edexcel's marking guidance there are plenty of mentions of an effective sales process as a way of answering other questions.

Here are 3 questions where the sales process and customer service are being tested. The first is an Edexcel question:

Q1. (From Paper 2. 2e) Explain one disadvantage to a business of providing poor customer service. (3)

Q2. A typical 6-mark question:

Discuss the benefits a business could gain from improving its sales process. (6 marks)

Q3. Carter's coffee shop has just opened at the entrance to a busy commuter railway station. Ruby Carter is deciding whether to focus most on speed of service or most on product quality.

Justify which one of these options Ms Carter should choose.   (9)

On the right are strong answers to these three questions. They are models for writing about the topic rather than how to score maximum marks.

For more on exam technique see Section 3.

Grade 9 Answers (questions on left)

Q1. A key disadvantage is the impact on the costs of the business. Loyal customers cost nothing to find; they find you. But if you lose customers (due to poor service), getting new ones is expensive (advertising or perhaps a new, better website).

Q2. *An improved sales process can boost revenue by increasing speed and efficiency. A City centre ice cream shop doesn't make money in the winter; but on a hot day queues form quickly. The faster the service, the more people you can serve – and the higher the revenues. The boost to revenues should boost profits, allowing the business to invest more – perhaps in better staff training and therefore even better service in future.*

Q3. In many locations this might be a difficult decision, but in this case speed of service is surely Number 1. Commuters won't return if getting a coffee makes them miss their train, so speed and efficiency is vital. It's also important for revenue, because customers will arrive at a similar time (before the train's due) so speed of service means getting more sales done in the window before the train arrives.

On the other hand if the coffee's on time but undrinkable, all but a few addicts will melt away. So the quality must be acceptable. Quality certainly means the taste, but also means the cup (not burning the customers' hands) and the quality of service. A quick 'Good morning' and a smile takes up no time.

Overall, though, the speed of service is likely to be the key to high revenues at this location.

Business Calculations

Percentages and Percentage change

A percentage is a hundredth, so 1% = one hundredth. If you need to find 20% of £8,400, multiply £8,400 by 20 hundredths, i.e. £8,400 $\times \frac{20}{100}$ = £1,680.

To calculate percentage change, use the formula: $\frac{\text{Change}}{\text{Original}} \times 100$

So if sales have risen from £420,000 to £483,000, the % increase is:

$\frac{\text{Change}}{\text{Original}} \times 100 = \frac{£63,000}{£420,000} \times 100 = +15\%$

Please answer these calculation questions. Answers are in the answer chapter.

1. Last year UK sales of Nutella were £50 million out of a total market of £325 million for 'Spreads'. What percentage did Nutella have of the market?

2. A company has set a target this year to increase its use of recycled materials from 21 tonnes to 35.7 tonnes. Calculate the percentage increase.

3. Last year's profit was £64,000; this year's profit is £56,320. Calculate the percentage change.

Averages

A business deals with lots of customers and collects lots of data – often in the form of numbers. To make sense of them it can help to use averages. Instead of knowing the age of each of those who buy a product online it helps to know that the average age is 52. Even more, if you have another product where the average age of buyers is 29. Your approach to marketing is likely to be quite different with 29-year-olds than with 52-year-olds.

Some questions:

4. Here are the gross profit margins for all 4 products made by the AXZ Company: Product A 27.5%; Product B 48%; Product C 37.5%; Product D 53%. Calculate the company's average gross profit margin.

5. On average only 1 new product in 5 is a financial success. Does that mean that if a company has 4 flops in a row it will be successful next time?

Gross and Net Profit Margin Ratios

A profit margin measures the profit as a percentage of the company's revenue. Gross profit is profit before deducting fixed overhead costs. Net profit is profit after the deduction of all operational costs including the cost of finance. The formulas are:

Gross profit margin = $\frac{\text{Gross profit}}{\text{Revenue}} \times 100$ Net profit margin = $\frac{\text{Net profit}}{\text{Revenue}} \times 100$

Q6. A business made £120,000 in gross profit last year from its £480,000 of revenue. Calculate its percentage gross profit margin.

Q7. This year the business expects to make a 30% gross margin on £600,000 of revenue. Calculate the expected gross profit total for the year.

Do really work on your calculations of % change. The chances of at least one question on this are about 99.5%. And you need this same skill in lots of other GCSE subjects as well.

Don't forget to show your workings when doing a calculation. But don't waste time writing down too much. The most important thing is the formula you're using. It helps the examiner but also helps you keep on track.

Exam tip: A profit margin is no more complicated than a percentage. The key is to separate gross margins from net margins. Gross are the big ones, i.e. before deducting the fixed operating costs.

Average rate of return

This is a way to estimate the possible profitability of an investment. The Average rate of return (ARR) shows the estimated annual profit on an investment as a percentage of the sum invested. If the ARR is calculated at 8% per year while bank interest rates are 3%, the investment provides a potential bonus of 5% a year above the safety of leaving money earning 3% interest at the bank.

To calculate ARR, use the formula: $\dfrac{\text{Average annual profit}}{\text{Sum invested}} \times 100$

For example, if a £100,000 investment looks likely to make £42,000 profit over a 3-year period, the ARR would be:

£42,000 / 3 years = £14,000 annual average profit per year

ARR = £14,000 / £100,000 x 100 = 14% a year.

Calculations

8. A business estimates that a £40,000 investment will generate a total profit of £32,000 over the next 4 years. Calculate the ARR.

9. At a time when bank interest rates were 6%, ACG Ltd estimated it could make a £24,000 profit over 6 years from the investment of £80,000. Calculate the ARR on the investment and suggest whether or not ACG Ltd should go ahead.

Other Business Calculation Questions

10. FG Co. has weekly sales of £16,000 from a product priced at £4 which has variable costs per unit of £1.60. Weekly fixed costs are £7,200.

10a) Calculate the break-even point

10b) Calculate the margin of safety

10c) Calculate FG Co's weekly profit.

11. Calculate the answers for 11a – 11f from this cash flow forecast

All figures in £000s	January	February	March	April
Opening balance	80	b)	75	90
Monthly cash inflow	55	70	85	e)
Monthly cash outflow	65	65	d)	120
Net cash flow	a)	c)	15	(30)
Closing balance	70	75	90	f)

Answers:

Q1. £50m/£325m x 100 = 15.4%

Q2. Increase = 14.7 tons
% increase = 14.7/21 x 100 = 70%

Q3. Change = - £7,680
% change = -£7,680/ £64,000 x 100 = -12%

Q4. Average = all 4 figures added up (166) divided by 4 = 41.5%

Q5. No, there's probably still a 1 in 5 chance next time. Averages work over time, but no single result is predictable.

Answers (cont)

Q6. Gross margin was £120,000 / £480,000 x 100 = 25%

Q7. This year's gross profit is £600,000 x 30/100 = £180,000

Q8. The £32,000 total profit = £32,000/4 = £8,000 per year. So the ARR is £8,000/£40,000 x 100 = 20%

9. The £24,000 total profit = £24,000/6 = £4,000 per year. So the ARR is £4,000/£80,000 x 100 = 5%. Might as well leave the money in the bank and earn a risk-free 6% a year.

Answers (cont)

Q10a) Break-even point = £7,200/£2.40 = 3,000

Q10b) Sales are £16,000/£4 = 4,000, so margin of safety is 4,000 - 3,000 = 1,000

10c) Weekly profit = £16,000 - (£7,200 + £6,400) = £2,400

11a) (£10,000)
11b) £70,000
11c) £5,000
11d) £70,000
11e) £90,000
11f) £60,000

Understanding Business Performance

Business Performance

At the heart of business performance are two figures and one method of comparison. Businesses care about the revenue generated from sales in a year, and the profit that has been made from that revenue. The comparison everyone makes is with the previous year's figures. A profit this year of £20 million may sound great – but if £40 million was made last year there will be more concern than delight.

To understand business performance you need to understand the numbers involved in generating profit. These include the marketing figures that affect the sales revenue the business generates, plus all the financial and other data involved in the total costs of the business.

Do digest the meaning of 'performance'. It's how well the business has performed at generating revenue and (especially) profit. And it's net profit that matters, not gross profit.

Information from graphs and charts

This graph shows the remarkable sales growth at Fever Tree plc, producers of 'mixers' such as tonic water. Look at the graph then answer the questions below.

Fever Tree plc: annual sales revenue

£millions

Source: Fever Tree accounts

Don't get put off by graphs or bar charts. The key is to read the title and the labels with care. So, on the left we can see Fever Tree's sales revenue (not profit) each year between 2005 and 2017, in £millions.

1. Calculate the percentage change in sales between 2015 and 2017.

2. Estimate the increase in sales revenue between 2008 and 2016.

3. How might this graph help a supermarket chain decide whether or not to stock Fever Tree products?

Exam tip: 10% of the marks come from quantitative skills. But these are an especially valuable 10%, because it's easier to get 10/10 on numbers than it is with written questions.

Financial Data

Financial data includes profit and loss, average rate of return and cash-flow forecasts. Of these three types of data, two are based on forecasts of what may happen in the future (ARR and cash-flow forecasts). If the business is in its first year of trading, these forecasts may be little more than guesses of what may happen. Therefore the results should be treated with great care. The profit and loss statement, by contrast, is likely to be a statement of what has already happened. For example, the profit may over the past 12 months. Things can go wrong with profit and loss data, but overall the figures are far more likely to be reliable.   **Some questions:**

4. After a net loss of £2 million last year, James is thrilled to announce a profit of £4 million this year. Revenue was £80 million last year and has risen to £100 million this year. The shareholders have set an average profit target of £2 million a year. How well has James done?

5. FR Ltd has 45 shops across the UK and is considering opening a 46th. Careful research and calculations have led the director to estimate the average rate of return at 12.5%. The business can fund the £250,000 investment from its own cash balances.

Should FR Ltd go ahead or not? Justify your answer.

Marketing data

Pringles have been researching a new flavour: Chilli Mango Salsa. The quantitative study has been carried out on 550 adults and here are the results to three key questions.

	Definitely will	Probably will	Not sure yes or no	Probably will not	Definitely not
Will you buy one pack to try?	26%	35%	21%	11%	7%
Do you expect to buy regularly?	11%	39%	18%	8%	24%
Will you buy instead of Pringle Salt & Vinegar?	12%	49%	24%	13%	2%

Are the following statements true or false?

6a) Most respondents said they will definitely or probably buy one pack to try.

6b) Nearly a quarter said they would definitely not buy regularly.

6c) 21% said they probably will not buy instead of Pringles Salt and Vinegar.

6d) There may be 550 interviews, but surely it's a waste of money to ask people who never eat Pringles.

Market data

Bosses care hugely about market share. If revenue is up but market share is down, questions will be asked. It's only possible to have rising revenue and falling market share if your competitors are doing better than you. If that happens one year, but you succeed in winning the share back next year, that's no problem. But when Nestle bought Rowntree in 1988 the combined business had a 29% share of the UK chocolate market. By 2017 that share had collapsed to 16%. That's a problem.

Q7. The UK market for skis is £2 million a year and your business sells £440,000 of that.

7a) Calculate your market share.

7b) Calculate the market share held by all your competitors.

7c) Is the figure you've calculated for 7b) a cause for concern?

Answers 1.
Q1. Change = +£109.7m
% change = +185%
Q2. 2016 is just over £100m, so the increase since 2008 seems to be approx. £100m.
Q3. Seeing this stunning growth, surely they'd want to stock Fever Tree asap.

Answers 2.
Q4. The average profit has been +£4m + -£2m/2 = £1 million a year James has failed to meet his profit target.
Q5. Yes. Because it's opening a 46th shop, they should be able to forecast accurately, so the 12.5% ARR looks good.

Answers 3.
Q6a) True
Q6b) True
Q6c) False
Q6d) True

Q7a) 22%
Q7b) 78%
Q7c) It might be if all 78% was controlled by one huge rival, but the questions talks of 'competitors' in the plural, so that's not the case. Businesses almost always have competition. It's not a cause for concern as long as the business has a competitive advantage.

Organisational structures

What? (Grade 5 basics)

The plan of who is answerable to whom in a business is known as the organisational structure. It sets out the layers of management, starting with the Chief Executive and going down to the 'shopfloor'. These are the horizontal layers of hierarchy. In a standard hierarchy, every individual has their own boss – set out on the diagram of organisational structure.

Why? (Grade 6)

There may be little need for a formal hierarchy in a small business, where everyone knows who manages whom. But in a massive business such as Tesco, with more than 250,000 staff, it can be helpful to see who is answerable to whom. If a young member of staff feels bullied by their supervisor, it's helpful to find out the supervisor's boss – to go to make a complaint. Then the bullying will stop. It's also great for junior staff to see the 'career ladder' – the promotion opportunities that may come their way in future.

How? (Grade 7)

To set out the hierarchy, there are two factors to consider: the vertical structure, e.g. how many management layers are there to be; and the horizontal structure, e.g. how many supervisors will be managed directly by a single boss. In some companies the average boss may be in charge of 4 people; in others the boss may have 8 or 9 under their control – a much bigger challenge.

So? (Grade 8)

In some businesses the hierarchy is flat, in other words not many layers of management. Each manager needs to be responsible for many junior staff (perhaps 10-12) because no supervisors are employed. This forces managers to trust their juniors, because they haven't got time to check up on everybody, all the time. This can work brilliantly if the junior staff seize their extra responsibility (think Google or Facebook) but some managers might find it stressful to be in direct charge of so many staff.

Grade 9

In 'centralised' organisations, bosses keep all the decision-making at the top of the hierarchy. Juniors are told what to do. In 'decentralised' organisations, many decisions are passed down to junior staff, to encourage them to get involved in management – and to find out which juniors deserve to be promoted. So organisational structure has a major impact on staff motivation.

Do consider which structure is most appropriate for the business in question. If the market is young and fast-growing, a flat structure will encourage fast decision-making by junior staff.

Don't assume there's one best organisational structure. It depends on the business. Young, growing businesses thrive on decentralised, flat structures. Older companies tend to develop tall hierarchies.

Exam tip: remember that a flat hierarchy works well with a decentralised approach. A taller hierarchy is likely to lead to a more centralised approach, keeping decisions at the top.

Organisational structure: 5-step logic chain (to get to the top level of response)

Chain 1. If a large business is struggling with market share it might consider a flatter organisational structure (1) ... to encourage younger staff to come up with new ideas (2) ... that may turn into profitable new products (3) When decisions are centralised at the top (4) ... they reflect the views of older, wealthy managers; those nearer the shopfloor are more tuned into ordinary people's tastes (5)

Chain 2. When a business has a highly profitable, stable brand it focuses on keeping things that way (1) ... and therefore focuses on avoiding mistakes (2). Therefore power is centralised (3) ... and a tall hierarchy is set up so that all ideas are checked by superiors (4) ... whose job is to avoid mistakes (5)

Importance of Effective Communications

What? (Grade 5 basics)

In a small business, everyone chats and everyone knows what's going on. So if the boss is out, others can help customers with a problem – or help clients wanting to place a big order. In large businesses this is harder, especially if many staff are part-timers or temps (temporary workers). So communication is an issue – and often a problem. Some people believe email has made things worse, with too few face-to-face meetings, and too many messages sent that are of no interest to many.

Why? (Grade 6)

The problem in a big business is there's so much going on that most people can only tune in to a small part. If I'm in charge of fresh fruit for Sainsbury in North-ampton, I may only be interested in my store plus the category I'm working in. So general emails flood into my Inbox – but leave me cold. Clever communication makes sure people only need to think about the things that matter to them.

How? (Grade 7)

The solution is to be selective. Excessive communication can be tough to wade through - tedious and stressful. But cutting back too much might mean a key message is missed. So bosses must filter out excess communication while making sure that individuals receive the information needed to do their job well. Even if the right messages are getting through, there can still be barriers to effective communication. Top bosses may use business-speak that junior staff can't follow. And if a junior is sending a message up through the hierarchy to the boss, it can get halted by a manager who can't see the importance of the complaint or idea.

So? (Grade 8)

It is important that top bosses see the value of effective communications throughout the business. Staff should be told that top bosses like to hear from the shopfloor, and middle managers should know never to block a message. And with electronic communication, selectivity is all-important.

Grade 9

In small businesses communication may be so easy and natural that no-one knows it can be 'a problem'. In bigger businesses it should always be on the mind of managers and bosses alike. Find a way to overcome communication barriers and you're a big step forward to being successful.

> **Do** think about the link between communications inside a business, and communic-ations outside, such as customers. Efficiency at one helps efficiency with the other.

> **Don't** assume that staff are at fault for failing to pick up key messages. It is the job of managers to make sure that staff know what they need to know. Some aren't good at that.

> **Exam tip**: Good communication doesn't mean lots of it. Show the examiner you understand how people today can get flooded with emails, perhaps struggling to focus on the important parts of their job.

Effective Communications: 5-step logic chain (to get to top level of response)

Chain 1. To give better customer service it's important to improve communications (1) … because a customer message that fails to get through can mean the wrong delivery is made (2) … wasting the company's money and the customer's time (3). This might end up with the customer looking elsewhere (4) … and finding a new, more efficient supplier that they choose to stay with (5).

Chain 2. Many businesses have their factory in one part of the country and the Headquarters somewhere else (usually London) (1) … which makes communication mistakes especially likely (2). So regular, face-to-face meetings are needed (3) … as it would be reckless to rely purely on email (4) … as so many staff complain that their Inboxes are too full to pick out the few important messages. (5)

Different Ways of Working

What? (Grade 5 basics)

Although people may think of a working life being based on a permanent, full-time job, there are other ways to work. Some part-timers have regular hours, such as 10.00 – 3.00 weekdays, so that kids can be taken to school. Others have irregular hours, flexible hours dictated by the employer. One week there's 20 hours' work, the next week nothing. This is OK for a young adult living at home, but not for a parent trying to pay regular bills such as the rent.

Why? (Grade 6)

Many businesses want a flexible workforce. Permanent, full-time staff work 35 hours when it's busy and 35 hours when things are slack. An efficient business wants to match working hours to the work needed. An ice cream factory may need to work 24/7 from May to August, but only for 5 hours a day in January and February. So the business may employ just a quarter of staff as permanent, full-timers and the remainder flexibly. Some temporary staff on 6-month contracts for the summer plus daily contract staff for when the weather's exceptional.

How? (Grade 7)

In the past, job contracts were pieces of paper setting out the hours and length of service. Now technology helps with more flexible arrangements. 'Remote' working (from home) risked losing contact with what's going on, but e-mail and Facetime now make it easy to avoid the boring commute. And Uber's App allows drivers to log in or out at any time, providing some flexibility for the business and the staff.

So? (Grade 8)

In an ideal world, the requirements of workers would be matched by the offers available from employers. Many people need the security of full-time, permanent jobs – but sometimes there aren't enough available. Perhaps more companies should care about hiring and keeping great people, and slightly less about flexibility. It may help those businesses have more motivated, more engaged staff.

Grade 9

In Business exams it's no problem to suggest that ethics should be a higher priority than profit. It's also reasonable to say that providing what staff need may boost morale and motivation. So why not let a parent go part-time, or give a young person wanting their first mortgage the chance of a full-time, permanent job? It may add to short-term costs, but build a more loyal workforce in the long term.

Do take care over the difference between temporary and freelance work. Freelance is being contracted to do a specific job, such as design a new website. Temporary work is being employed for a fixed period, e.g. a month.

Don't doubt the importance of technology, not just for remote working but also the speed and efficiency with which Apps can match people to the jobs that need to be done. The Uber approach may be the future.

Exam tip: examiners love a two-sided answer. Here, it's easy. Flexible working has clear advantages and disadvantages, both for the individual and the business.

Different ways of working: 5-step logic chain (to get to top level of response)

Chain 1. Many businesses have seasonal demand and therefore can't be efficient if everyone is on a permanent contract (1) … so there is a proper business case for flexible working (2). Some businesses seize the opportunity to create a job in which holiday pay and pensions don't need to be paid for (3)… which seems like exploitation (4). Trade union membership is one way staff can protect themselves (5)

Chain 2. Flexible contracts can be great for young people (1) … especially if they can work long hours one week, then take the next week off (2). So flexible working isn't all bad (3) … especially if there's flexibility on both sides (4). What feels wrong is a situation where the flexibility works really well for the business, but at the expense of the security of a family. (5)

Effective Recruitment

What? (Grade 5 basics)

Before recruiting, businesses must identify the job roles and responsibilities they need. Directors may be in place, but as the business expands they may need a new layer of senior managers. These new roles need to be created to help make future plans successful. When recruiting senior managers, the business may look for internal candidates or for people outside the business (external recruitment).

Why? (Grade 6)

Effective recruitment needs a clear idea about the personal qualities needed by staff in different job roles. Company directors need the experience and talent to make decisions about the long-term future of the business. Managers, team leaders and supervisors need to be able to organise and motivate staff towards the achievement of clear targets. And operational and support staff need to work hard and intelligently, but under the direction of their supervisors.

How? (Grade 7)

Having identified the need for a new recruit, two documents are needed. A job description sets out the tasks and responsibilities of the job; and a person specification identifies the qualifications, experience and personality of the ideal recruit. Applicants for the job will need to fill out an application form and provide a C.V. – a written statement by each candidate about their background, achievements and ambitions. Then the selection process can take place.

So? (Grade 8)

If you run a business that is growing well and making good profits, it makes sense to recruit internally. The person who already works for you knows and understands the business – and will therefore be able to work well straight away. And internal promotions help motivate other staff – and make them less likely to look for jobs elsewhere. Whereas businesses in crisis are likely to look outside – for an external candidate with fresh ideas.

Grade 9

So, depending on the business situation, you might either recommend a search for someone completely new – who can shake things up and force existing staff to re-think their attitudes and behaviours. Or recommend an internal candidate who can keep the ship sailing steadily on the same course. It depends on the circumstances of the business at that time (which you get from the text).

> **Do** think about recruitment from the point of view of the business. Companies want people who are reliable, keen, willing to learn and work well with others.

> **Don't** lump directors and managers together. Directors set the long-term objectives and strategies. Managers have to make them happen, using the staff available to them.

> **Exam tip**: examiners ask a lot of questions about internal & external recruitment. Prepare by thinking about two or three of your favourite – and least favourite – shops. Should they be recruiting externally? Why, exactly?

Effective Recruitment: 5-step logic chain (to get to top level of response)

Chain 1. SuperDry has been expanding steadily and successfully using internal recruitment (1) ... for all jobs above the shopfloor level, such as supervisors and managers (2). This helps in developing a consistent way of working throughout management (3) ... which in turn makes it easier for supervisors to become managers (4). For new shopfloor staff, external recruitment is needed (5).

Chain 2. To be effective, recruitment must lead to the right type of people being hired (1) ... such as outgoing, friendly staff to work in a coffee shop or bar (2). Happy, chatty staff boosts customer service (3) ... which can lead to more customer loyalty/repeat business (4) ... boosting the company's revenue and profits. (5)

Effective Training and Development

What? (Grade 5 basics)

There are many different ways of training and developing employees. 'Formal' training includes all the plans businesses have to develop staff, such as regular weekly sessions for all. Some shops open an hour later one day a week so that staff get an hour's training.

Many businesses set targets for staff at the beginning of the year, then agree the extra training needed to help staff meet those targets. At the end of the year, a 'performance review' gives a one-to-one discussion with a manager about whether the targets have been met. Often informal training is even more important, with new recruits learning from others about what to do and how to do it.

Why? (Grade 6)

Staff like to feel comfortable in their knowledge – to be able to answer customer questions or solve their problems. So expertise matters – and training is the obvious way to provide it. Well-trained staff are more likely to be motivated in their job and far less likely to look around for a new job. So staff 'retention' increases; more staff stay in their job.

With technology developing rapidly, it's also vital to re-train staff to help keep on top of changes. In future staff may be working more with robots and 'intelligent' machines – and will need to learn how to do this. Retraining to use new technology will be an increasing part of everyone's working life.

How? (Grade 7)

Effective training starts with an understanding of what matters most to customers. If they want a fun, upbeat experience, then staff must be trained to provide exactly that. In other cases, the key may be intense training on new software systems – to ensure that customers' online ordering is quick, easy and accurate. In the best businesses, senior managers care about training, making sure that time and money is available for exciting but relevant activities.

So? (Grade 8)

With sports stars people are tempted to talk about 'natural' abilities. Read the diary of a sports star and it soon becomes clear that the 'natural' gifts emerged after hours and hours of training and practice. Great training makes people confident and helps their work and skills seem effortless. This makes it easy for them to make customers feel special.

Grade 9

Despite these positives, companies in the UK are among the meanest in Europe at paying for high quality training. It seems that they'd rather pay out higher dividends to shareholders than spend the company's money on their staff. If the business in the exam is one that does spend heavily on training, it deserves praise. And that business may have a huge long-term advantage over rivals that spend less on training. This is a great way to establish a competitive advantage.

Do remember the terms 'formal' and 'informal' training. They work well with examiners. Formal training must be organised – and paid for – by the business. Luckily informal training takes place everywhere – and at no cost to the company.

Don't expect too much from target setting and performance reviews. Research shows that staff are far more motivated by regular chats with and praise from bosses than by once-a-year meetings.

Exam tip: in the Specification, the key phrases for exam questions are: 'the link between training, motivation and retention' and 'retraining to use new technology'. Expect these to lead to 6, 9 or 12 mark questions.

Training & Development: 5-step logic chain (getting to the top response level)

Chain 1. A business with poor productivity needs to spend more on training (1) … partly to improve the technical skills of staff and therefore boost their efficiency (2) … and partly to make staff feel better looked after by the business, which can help with motivation (3). That, in turn, can help boost productivity (4) … due to better, trained technique plus better morale and therefore effort (5).

Chain 2. Many businesses provide plenty of training for middle and senior managers, but too little for shopfloor operational staff (1). This risks undermining motivation and retention among junior staff (2) … which in the long run damages the company's ability to develop and promote staff internally (3). So the business recruits managers from outside the business (4) … who may just stay for a year or two before leaving for a better-paid job elsewhere. (5).

Answering exams

Here are 3 questions where training and development are being tested. The first is an Edexcel question, the other two are in the Edexcel style:

Q1. (From Paper 2. 1d) Explain one advantage to a business of providing ongoing training to its employees. (3)

Q2. A typical 6-mark question:

Discuss the benefits a business could gain from the use of target setting and performance reviews. (6 marks)

Q3. A new director at VX Printing wants to halve the £100,000 budget for staff training. The training manager says it's a mistake, risking staff motivation and retention.

Justify which one of these two possibilities would be most damaging to the business. (9)

On the right are strong answers to these three questions (though the Q3 answer is overly short – there just wasn't enough space).

Grade 9 Answers (questions on left)

Q1. Regular (ongoing) training sessions help build a higher level of understanding of what is wanted. In sport there's a term 'muscle memory' implying the muscles know what to do without being told. Ongoing training should do the same, e.g. knowing how to deal with a tricky situation without thinking about it.

Q2. Ambitious people want to know how to get to the next level, e.g. a promotion. If set targets at the beginning of the year they'll focus on meeting then beating them. So they'll work consistently hard, looking forward to the end-of-year performance review, certain that their boss will be impressed. The business will enjoy higher productivity which helps to reduce costs per unit produced and therefore profit.

However, other people may respond better if a manager offered more support and praise more regularly. These people may struggle to care about a discussion that might take place many months' away.

Q3. The more serious is probably retention. If staff are always leaving it's hard to build up knowledge of what's special about the business. That makes it hard for customers to see much that's special. And if retention is low, there are so many new, inexperienced staff always joining that productivity will be low, which pushes up costs and cuts into profits. On the other hand, low retention guarantees new people and ideas

Motivation

What? (Grade 5 basics)

Staff motivation is important to keep productivity and retention high. It also helps in attracting top young talent, if word spreads that this is a great place to work. Motivation comes about when individuals feel confident that their abilities and achievements are recognised. So managers have a big role to play: to give staff a task with enough challenge for their talents to show through – and then to see who's rising to that challenge.

Why? (Grade 6)

Many managers think it's enough for staff to give 'a fair day's work for a fair day's pay'. But – just like school students – most staff could put twice as much effort and thought into their work, if they really wanted to. Motivated staff do exactly that. They don't work down to the average effort involved in a 'fair day's work', they do their best. Just like the footballer who gives '110%' and clearly just loves playing. There are few more important topics in business than human motivation.

How? (Grade 7)

Businesses 'motivate' employees in two ways. Most of the ways used by managers aren't really about motivation at all – they are about incentives. Financial incentives include bonuses, commission, the promise of promotion and fringe benefits such as a company car. These forms of remuneration provide a target that many staff will try to achieve. To motivate staff, though, it's better to create a more interesting, challenging job ('job enrichment') or to give staff more 'autonomy', i.e. the ability to make their own decisions without needing to get them checked out by their boss. A further non-financial approach is 'job rotation', which can mean little more than swapping tasks to relieve boredom, e.g. the check-out operator spends a couple of hours stacking shelves and another hour or two on the fish counter.

So? (Grade 8)

If you look at the difference between Number 1 and Number 2 in the Premier League or in cafes in your High Street, the explanation is often motivation. Not that staff are paid more, but because they care more – they have a passion and therefore an energy that has been turned into success. This can be due to an inspirational leader: an Elon Musk or a Pep Guardiola, but is often because staff have been given autonomy, and trusted by being given responsibility.

Grade 9

Years ago business was largely about manufacturing. So motivation mattered most in terms of productivity: making 20 chocolate bars a minute instead of 16. Today 80% of the UK economy is based on services: from making TV programmes to selling clothes in-store or online. So a vital part of motivation today is getting great, creative ideas from staff. You want them feeling involved enough to pass on ideas to their bosses. Japanese car giant Toyota is resisting the move to robot production because they value staff ideas too much to replace staff with robots.

Do remember the short list of benefits from motivation identified by Edexcel:

- attracting employees,
- retaining employees
- productivity.

Don't confuse job rotation and job enrichment. Job rotation means swapping tasks, usually of the same degree of difficulty. Job enrichment is about the job having more challenges as well as a greater variety of tasks.

Exam tip 1: examiners love business words, so learn the definition of 'remuneration', 'commission', 'autonomy' and 'fringe benefits'.

Exam tip 2: If you can link motivation to productivity, it's easy then to relate it to keeping costs down and therefore gaining a competitive advantage.

Motivation: 5-step logic chain (getting to the top response level)

Chain 1. When a bright new manager gives staff more autonomy and responsibility (1) … it can spark a boost to productivity (2) … which helps bring costs per unit down and efficiency up (3) … which helps provide the business with a competitive advantage (4) … which may help it succeed not only in the UK but also in overseas markets (5).

Chain 2. The super-successful businesses such as Google pay great salaries with amazing fringe benefits (1) … not to motivate staff but to retain them (2) … and to attract the best and brightest from the best universities (3). For motivation they rely on providing autonomy on the work itself (4) … giving staff the opportunity to make their name with a brilliant new product idea. (5).

Answering exams

Here are 3 questions where motivation is being tested. The first two are Edexcel questions, the last one is in the Edexcel style:

Q1. (From Paper 2. 3c) Explain one reason why a business may decide to pay its workers a bonus. (3)

Q2. (From Paper 2. 3d):
Explain one drawback to a business of not being able to retain its employees.(3)

Q3. Tesco wants to improve staff motivation. It sees two options: Option1 is to use non-financial methods and Option 2 is to use financial methods.

Justify which one of these two options you recommend.   (9)

On the right are strong answers to these three questions. They are models for writing about the topic rather than models for how to score 3 or 9 marks.

For more on exam technique see Section 3.

Grade 9 Answers (questions on left)

Q1. It may pay a bonus in order to focus staff on a key objective, such as cutting food wastage. Achieving this will cut variable costs and therefore cut the break-even point – as long as the bonus isn't too big.

Q2. When a new member of staff starts, it takes many weeks to reach full effectiveness. At the start they're asking more questions than doing anything useful. If you can't retain your employees you keep needing to hire new staff. And their inefficiency would hit productivity.

Q3. To motivate staff non-financial methods should be chosen. Tesco wants enthusiastic staff who are helpful to customers, so job enrichment is the way forward. This would give jobs with a wider range of tasks and responsibilities. That provides more challenge and therefore more interest in the work – and hopefully more commitment to customers' needs and wants.

On the other hand staff at Tesco may be so used to doing the same low-level tasks day-in day-out that they may be worried, even stressed, by being offered more responsibility. In the long term job enrichment is the way forward, but perhaps in the short term it would be disruptive – causing a jolt to labour retention.

Tesco should test out any changes in one or two stores before deciding on what to do next.

Mastering Application

Problem 1.

Examiners want to do more than test your knowledge of business. They want to know what you can <u>do</u> with that knowledge. Can you weigh up a business problem or opportunity based on a real business situation? That's the skill of application. You applying your mind to a specific business situation – the one the examiner has chosen to write about. The problem is that students skim read the text, rushing to get to the questions.

The Solution

Read the text with care; try to read actively. Think about what's being said or hinted at. Make brief notes in the margin – that's a usefully active thing to do. Don't use a highlighter; that's too passive. And when you've finished reading, jot down what you *feel* about the story. That's important because what you feel is really your judgement. And that links application with another important skill – evaluation. Having read a business story you might feel: 'Risky!' 'Wow, brilliant!' 'Running before they can walk??' or 'Better watch the cash flow'. All these would be likely to lead to fabulous application.

Problem 2.

Time after time, examiners report that student answers ignore the business context. If the exam material is about *Missguided*, their answers simply mention *Missguided* occasionally. But that's not the point.

The Solution

When reading the short piece about a business, ask yourself: 'what's <u>distinctive</u> or special about this particular company?' Your job is to use that information to answer an exam question such as:

'Analyse the benefits *Missguided* might gain from selling shop franchises.' (6)

Instead of getting lost in explaining the benefits of franchising, a good answer will wrap those benefits around *Missguided*'s distinctive characteristics.

Problem 3.

So how do you decide what's distinctive? The answer is anything that strikes you, i.e. <u>your</u> thoughts are crucial. As long as you can justify why a point is distinctive, the examiner will go along with you.

The Solution

Read this business start-up story and identify 3 distinctive features:

'Den and girlfriend Pam started PD Ltd. with £15,000 borrowed from a friend and £15,000 from HSBC. Both keen surfers, their plan was to open the first surfing school in the North East, on the coast above Newcastle. They were confident that they could persuade the Geordies to take up surfing, despite the cold weather.'

Now, what did you feel after reading this text? Perhaps 'daft idea' or 'that'll never work' which ideally you'd translate into business-speak: 'Risky!' You might have picked out the risky financing (debt); the importance of the word 'first' – which can be used to build an argument for and an argument against this business idea. You might have picked up on 'keen surfers' – suggesting that their enthusiasm might rub off, giving customers a great experience. The point is it doesn't matter what you select – as long as you pick on one or two distinctive points and build a business argument around them.

> **Do** jot down points in the margin as you read through the text. Highlighters aren't as effective. And practise short conclusions at the end of the text, based on what you feel, i.e. your gut instinct. And use that to build arguments: 'I think it's too risky because ...'

> **Don't** lose sight of the business story as you work through your answer. On a 9-mark question it's important to make a full reference to the business situation in all 3 sections of your answer: the case for, the counter-argument and the judgement.

> **Exam tip:** be bold not timid. If you think a new product idea seems weak, say so (but you have to explain *why* you say that). Strong opinions matter, though don't ignore the counter-argument. I love Marmite, but I can see why others hate it.

Mastering Time: In The Exam Itself

Problem 1.

In all exams students tend to write too much at the start. Nerves are fizzing away and the response to the first questions is to write plenty – to make sure of the marks. Big mistake. The time is needed later.

The Solution

Be self-disciplined. Force yourself to be brief on the early questions. These aren't the questions that will really matter for grades. They're coming later.

Problem 2.

Re-writing the question. This is the ultimate in time-wasting. The examiner knows the question – you don't need to rewrite it. So if there's a question such as 'Explain **one** benefit to employees of employment law' (3 marks), most answers start with "One benefit to employees of employment law ...". These words may only waste a quarter of a minute, but as there are about 16 written questions per exam paper, that's 4 minutes wasted. That could be the difference between having 7 minutes and 11 minutes to answer a 9-mark question.

The Solution

Start answering the question straight away. In answer to that question on employment law, dive in: 'The law sets a minimum standard such as the National Living Wage. As all employees have to be paid at or above that level it helps reduce poverty and therefore reduced inequality.'

Problem 3.

You may know too much – and want the examiner to know how much you know. Also a big mistake. All the examiner cares about is whether you know how to answer the questions set.

The Solution

Again, self-discipline is needed. You may know loads about cash flow, but if the question is about profit, don't stray for a second. In this case attempting to show off your knowledge about cash flow will actually harm your mark – but it suggests to the examiner that you don't know the difference between these two concepts.

Every sentence you write must be focused directly at the question set. The *precise* wording of the question. Take a look at these two answers to the question:

Explain **one** disadvantage to a small business of using an overdraft as a source of finance. (3)

Tight focus on the question	Answer focused poorly on question
An overdraft is on 24 hours' recall, so the bank can demand that the debt be repaid in full within a day. A small business is unlikely to be able to find the funds needed, raising the threat of insolvency	One disadvantage to a small business is that the bank may want the overdraft repaid in 24 hours. It's better if the business has a bank loan because that's for a set period of time, such as 2 years. Crowdfunding would also be a better and safer way to get capital for a small business.

Commentary: on the left is a nice, quick 3 marks out of 3. On the right is a long-winded 1 mark out of 3.

Do practise writing answers with 'connective' words such as because, as, therefore, 'so that' and however. And with a 12-mark question, the conclusion is improved by the magic words: 'It depends.'

Don't try to answer an exam paper in a different order, e.g. the 12-mark questions first. Examiners use 2 and 6-mark questions to get you used to the business story. Then you'll write better answers to the tougher questions.

Exam tip: if, despite your best efforts, you have only 6 minutes left for the final, 12-mark question, don't start to write in note-form or bullet points. Write your case For, making clear references to the business situation and build your 5-step analysis.

Mastering Time: Written Questions

The Problem

Edexcel has been very mean with the time given to these exams. 90 marks in 90 minutes gives a maximum of 10 minutes' reading time, then 80 minutes for 90 marks. In truth, that's long enough for candidates who aren't able to answer every question. But it's very tough on those who have plenty to think about and plenty to say – the better candidates, in other words.

The Solution

The most important way to save time in an exam is to keep short answers short. 3-mark questions need to be answered in 2 minutes, perhaps even one-and-a-half. Where thinking time is needed is when answering 9 or 12-mark questions.

Question 7 of Edexcel's First Specimen Paper 1 has 3 very short questions. They stem from a start-up story about Sally, a fitness instructor going it alone to operate a personal trainer business.

7 (a) State one risk that Sally faces in starting this business. (1)

ANS: Losing her savings

Commentary: no need for a full sentence; just quickly state your point.

7b) Identify which of Sally's competitors is the most expensive per hour. (1)

ANS: Competitor 1.

Commentary: a quick bit of mental arithmetic was required (or a quick calculation) but in this case don't show workings, there's only 1 mark at stake – and this answer gets it.

7c) Outline one way in which the economic climate might impact on Sally's business. (2)

ANS: Falling consumer incomes are a concern as Sally charges higher prices than both fitness competitors (1); this may damage her market share and profit (1).

Commentary: the 2-mark question is hard to keep really short – but this answer comfortably scores 2 marks as the second part is linked to the first.

From Edexcel's second set of Specimen Papers comes this.

1c) Explain one risk an entrepreneur takes when starting a new business. (3)

ANS: One risk is wiping out a lifetime's savings (1). A slow start to trading can eat into reserves of capital (1). If customer numbers stay below break-even, the business may close - wiping out the owner's savings (1).

Commentary: with 'Explain' questions, make a point then build on it – twice.

Problem 2.

The other big problem is how to condense an answer to a 9-mark question into 8-9 minutes. You first have to read and master a piece of text about a real business. Then the question offers 2 options as possible solutions to a problem. You must choose one then weigh up its pros and cons in relation to the business. Then reach a judgement.

Do be willing to answer short questions in phrases rather than sentences. But make sure that each phrase follows on from the one before. 'So', 'because' and 'therefore' are powerful words.

Don't waste time with a first sentence that repeats the question. And only start with a definition when answering a 12-mark question. For the 9-markers in particular, definitions waste time without scoring marks.

Exam tip: with short questions, it's OK to lose an occasional mark by being too brief. Top grades depend on the 9 and 12-mark questions, so it's vital to create some time to do them really well.

Solution 2.

A good way to save time is to be very focused on 3 things: For, Against, & Judgement, or FAJ for short. When you read through the text, make brief notes in the margin. These should include you writing in F or A as you see points for or against the business. When you get to the end, write a brief Judgement, e.g. 'Risky!!' or 'Great idea' or 'Short of cash'.

Take the following text from a past Edexcel exam paper:

'Mark Steel is a qualified hairdresser looking to set up in business as a sole trader. He has carried out some market research in the town where he lives. There are 11 hairdressing businesses in the town. Mark's speciality is in creating styles which involve a high degree of skill that adds significant value. Mark's reputation has been boosted by winning a styling competition in a leading fashion magazine.'

Without looking at the exam questions it's possible to add in F, A and J as you read. You'd come up with something like:

'Mark Steel is a qualified ⬚F hairdresser looking to set up in business as a sole ⬚A trader. He has carried out ⬚F some market research in the town where he lives. There are 11 hairdressing ⬚A businesses in the town. Mark's speciality is in creating styles which involve a high degree of skill that ⬚F adds significant value. Mark's reputation has been boosted by winning a styling ⬚F competition in a leading fashion magazine.' ⬚ J = Looks promising

> **Commentary:**
> there are four clear points in favour of Mark's start-up. 3 of them overlap in relation to his credentials and their potential value, including the opportunity to push prices up. The 4th is his use of market research – showing a business-like approach.

Reading and making such brief notes will help save time. You won't need to re-read the text. Then use the same FAJ approach when answering the 9-mark question: 1. Choose the option you favour. 2. Put a strong case For, making clear reference to the business context 3. Put a slightly less strong case Against 4. Make a Judgement in favour – explaining why.

To make the same case again, but setting it out more clearly for a 9-mark answer:

	Approximate mark target	Implied timing	Advice
Case For	4 marks	4 minutes	No need to cover more than one point, but develop it fully (remember 5-point analysis)
Case Against	3 marks	3 minutes	No need to cover more than one point, but develop it fully
Judgement	2 marks	2 minutes	Explain clearly why you think the argument for outweighs the argument against

> **Do** remember that 5-point analysis doesn't have to be achieved in one go. 3-point analysis in the case For plus 2-point analysis in the case Against still gets you to the top level for analysis.

Conclusion

Time is super-tight, but if you keep focused, keep working and follow these two rules you'll be fine: keep short answers short; and when reading the text and answering the longer questions, follow this simple approach: FAJ (For, Against & Judgement).

Mastering Time: Calculating Profit

The Normal Method

All students are taught that Revenue – Total Costs = Profit. Quite right. But the calculation is quite lengthy and therefore slow. And therefore bad news in a tightly timed exam. So, as long as you're reasonably confident with numbers, use the formula your teachers keep to themselves. It's their short-cut.

All you need to know for the shortcut is contribution per unit, a formula you need for calculating break-even.

The shortcut formula is: Profit = Total contribution – Fixed costs

Trust me, it's much quicker. You can why from this example.

A business sells 2,000 units a week at £6 each. Its variable costs are £4 per unit and fixed costs are £2,500 a week. Calculate the profit.

Using Total Revenue – Total costs	Using Total Contribution – Fixed Costs
Total revenue = Price x Quantity	Total contribution = (Price – V.C.p.u.) x Quantity
Total revenue = £6 x 2,000 = £12,000	Total contribution = (£6-£4) x 2,000 = £4,000
Total costs = Total variable costs + Fixed costs	Profit = £4,000 - £2,500 = **£1,500 ANS**
Total variable costs = £4 x 2,000 = £8,000	
Total costs = £8,000 + £2,500 = £10,500	
Profit = £12,000 - £10,500 = **£1,500 ANS**	

> **Do** show the examiner what you're doing. The examiner will know your contribution formula, so set it out clearly and you'll get an instant mark.

The above table shows how the contribution short-cut saves a huge amount of calculation – and all that calculation is taking time.

This time, I've done the long-winded method; you do the quick way – and check against my answer. Sales are 250 units a week at £30 each; variable costs per unit are £18 and weekly fixed costs are £2,200.

Using Total Revenue – Total costs	Using Total Contribution – Fixed Costs
Total revenue = Price x Quantity	
Total revenue = £30 x 250 = £7,500	
Total costs = Total variable costs + Fixed costs	
Total variable costs = £18 x 250 = £4,500	
Total costs = £4,500 + £2,200 = £6,700	
Profit = £7,500 - £6,700 = **£800 ANS**	

> **Don't** switch to the contribution method of calculating profit unless you've had plenty of practice. Use the questions here and also ask your teacher for more profit calculations – always tackling them using contribution.

More practice questions – answer using contribution only

1. Sales are 150 units a day, price is £40, variable costs p.u. £28 & fixed costs £800 a day. 1a) Calculate current profit. 1b) Calculate new profit if sales rise by 50 units.

2. Sales are 600 units a day, price is £50, variable costs p.u. £30 & fixed costs £7,500 a day. Calculate: 2a) Break-even output 2b) The margin of safety and 2c) Current profit.

3. Sales are 40 units a day, price is £20, variable costs p.u. £6 & fixed costs £400 a day. 3a) Calculate current profit. 3b) Calculate new profit if variable costs fall to £4 a unit.

> **Answers:**
> 1a) £1,000
> 1b) £1,600
> 2a) 375 units
> 2b) 225 units
> 2c) £4,500
> 3a) £160
> 3b) £240

Grade 9 Exam Technique

Problem 1.

Getting the basics right within very tight timings. 90 minutes for 90 marks is far too little time for a strong candidate. Those with plenty of knowledge write too much on early questions and run out of time.

The Solution

Accept the time constraint. This isn't a test of who knows most about Business. It's about who can write the best answers to 90 marks of Business questions within the very tight timing: 90 minutes. Think about the arguments you construct – and count 1–5 as you go through a chain of logic. Or, if you're running short of time: write a 1,2,3 chain in your case For and 1,2 in the case Against before making and justifying your Judgement. The 5-step logic chain can be split over two sides. This will save time.

Problem 2.

Getting from Level 2 (4-6 marks) to Level 3 (7-9 marks) on the 9-mark question.

The Solution

Choose one option and build the case for and against that option. There's no need to refer to the other option (though you might in your evaluation, if it seemed helpful).

The key to Level 3 is a justified decision/recommendation. Don't sit on the fence. Make a decision and justify it.

On Edexcel's mark scheme for the 9-marker, three things separate Level 3 from Level 2. To get to Level 3:

- Application must be shown 'throughout' the answer. So remember to refer to the business within all three phases of your answer: the argument, the counter-argument and the evaluation (decision plus justification)
- Level 3 analysis requires 'detailed, interconnected points within your 5-step chain of reasoning. So it's not enough to say 'cutting costs will increase profit', you'd need: 'cutting fixed costs boosts the vertical gap between total costs and total revenue on a break-even chart, therefore increasing profit.'
- A Level 3 conclusion needs to be well-reasoned based on 'thorough' evaluation of business information and issues 'relevant to the choice made'.

Problem 3.

Getting from Level 2 (5-8 marks) to Level 3 (9-12 marks) on the 12-mark question.

The Solution

On Edexcel's mark scheme for the 12-marker, three things separate Level 3 from Level 2. To get to Level 3:

- Application must be shown 'throughout' the answer. So remember to refer back to the business within your counter-argument and your conclusion (as well as in your original argument)
- Level 3 analysis requires your 5-step chain of reasoning to be more detailed. This would be helped by building your chain of reasoning using relevant business concepts, e.g. motivation linked to productivity linked to unit costs
- A Level 3 conclusion needs to be well-reasoned based on 'thorough' evaluation of business information/issues, implying 5-6 lines of conclusion.

Do be willing to be bold. A Grade 9 answer should stand out, therefore a bold decision or conclusion can help. And when you know you're being bold you also know you have to find a very convincing argument to justify your point. That forces you to think hard.

Don't worry about Edexcel's ruled lines for the answers. High-mark answers are usually a lot longer than the Board expects. If you have the time, keep writing your answer. Feel happy to write outside the Board's lines – they'll mark it!

Exam tip: don't worry about showing off all your knowledge (including all those definitions). If you're answering the questions directly the examiner will see how bright you are – and give you the top marks you deserve.

Answers to Numerical Questions

1.3.2a) Revenue and costs

Q1a) DF Ltd monthly sales revenue

Quantity x Price = Revenue

  800   x £8   = **£6,400**

Q1b) DF Ltd total costs

Total variable costs + Fixed costs = Total costs

  (800 units x £2)   +   £1,500   = **£3,100**

Q2a) Revenue per flight

Number of passengers x Flight price = Revenue per flight

(120 passengers x £50) + (80 x £90) = £6,000 + £7,200 = **£13,200**

Q2b) Total costs

Total variable costs + Fixed costs = Total costs

(200 passengers x £5) + £9,200   = **£10,200**

Q3a) Weekly revenue

(500 cakes x £2) + (600 loaves x £2.50) = **£2,500**

Q3b) Total variable costs + Fixed costs = Total costs

So: (1,100 units x £1)   +   ?   = £2,100

Answer = £2,100 - £1,100 = **£1,000**

Q4a) If Quantity x Price = Revenue

Then Quantity = Revenue / Price

£15,000 / £30 = **500 surfers**

Q4b) If total costs are £12,500 of which £5,000 are fixed, then £7,500 is the total variable cost. So variable costs per hour are £7,500 / 500 surfers = **£15 an hour**

1.3.2b) Profit and Loss

Q1a) BGT Ltd weekly profit/loss

Total Revenue   -   Total Costs   = Profit

(100 x £25) − ([100 x £10] + £900)   =

     £2,500   -   £1,900   = **£600**

Q1b) BGT Ltd weekly profit/loss if sales double

Total Revenue   -   Total Costs   = Profit

  (200 x £25) − ([200 x £10] + £900)   =

     £5,000   -   £2,900   = **£2,100**

Do make sure to set out the formula you're using to answer maths questions. It helps the examiner, but much more importantly it helps you structure your answer. That makes mistakes much less likely.

Don't forget that fixed costs can change. Rents can rise and interest rates can rise or fall. The thing about fixed costs is they're fixed in relation to output.

Exam tip: maths questions will be 10% of the marks on each exam paper. But they're a hugely important 10%. If you're good at them, 10/10 is a serious possibility. While others will be getting 0/10. That makes maths questions a big swing factor in getting grades.

Answers to Numerical Questions

Q2. A clothes store's weekly profit

Revenue: (400 x £15) + (250 x £4)   = £7,000

Variable costs (400 x £4) + (250 x £2) = £2,100

Profit = £7,000 – (£2,100 + £1,200)   = **£3,700**

Q3. The farmer's strawberries

3a) Weekly total costs: (5,000 kilos x £0.40p = £2,000) + £6,500 = **£8,500**

3b) Weekly profit = £10,000 - £8,500 = **£1,500**

Q4a) Number of surfers = £24,000 / £30 = **800 surfers**

Q4b) Profit = Revenue £24,000 – Total costs £15,000 = **£9,000**

Q4c) New profit = Revenue £36,000 – (£16,000 variable + £7,000 fixed) = **£13,000 profit**

> **Don't** panic if Edexcel has forced you to calculate revenue or costs for two products. The principles remain exactly the same.

1.3.3 Cash Flow

1. BVK Ltd

If the net cash flow this month is £33,000 - £30,000 = +£3,000 …

… and there's a closing balance of +£10,000

… then the month's opening balance must have been **+£7,000**

2a) Clothing business cash flow

a) £300

b) £3,300

c) £7,000

d) -£3,000

e) -£3,900

2b) It's only possible if the business has a big enough overdraft agreed with the bank.

> **Don't** be surprised if you have to complete a cash flow table. Examiners love it because it's so easy to mark!

3. Might be incorrect because the sales forecast proved to be wrong – which is almost inevitable for a new business. However much was spent on market research, you could never be certain about the number of customers for a new business.

Could also be incorrect because of competitors' responses to your opening. In such a cut-throat sector as pizza delivery (with huge rivals such as Domino's) unexpectedly sharp price cutting by rivals may dent your customer numbers (and threaten your ability to survive the difficult early months)

> **Exam tip:** even with finance questions remember the business context. Here, it's easy to make references to the pizza market.